How to DISCIPLE your Children

Walter A. Henrichsen

While this book is designed for the reader's personal enjoyment and profit, it is also intended for group study. A Leader's Guide with Victor Multiuse Masters is available from your local bookstore or from the publisher.

D0391421

VICTOR

V ™

BOOKS a division of SP Publications, Inc.
WHEATON. ILLINOIS 60187

Offices also in
Whitby, Ontario, Canada
Amersham-on-the-Hill, Bucks, England

**Cover Illustration
by Louis Cuevas**

Third printing, 1983

Most of the Scripture quotations in this book are from *The New International Version* (NIV), © 1978 by The New York International-al Bible Society. Other quotations are from the King James Version (KJV) and *The Living Bible* (LB), © by Tyndale House Publishers, Wheaton, Ill. All are used by permission of the publishers.

Recommended Dewey Decimal Classification: 248.82
Suggested subject heading: CHILDREN—CHRISTIAN LIFE

LIBRARY OF CONGRESS CATALOG CARD NUMBER: 80-52905
ISBN: 0-88207-260-9

VICTOR BOOKS
A division of SP Publications, Inc.
P.O. Box 1825   ●   Wheaton, Illinois 60187

Dedicated
to my wife and four children
Deborah Lynn
Walter
Jonathan
Janna Kay
one of whom, at the time of this writing, has
entered into the presence of Jesus.
These five, more than my many mentors, have
taught me what I know about the Christian life.

CONTENTS

FOREWARD

Walt Henrichsen has written a book that is destined to provide practical help for many a modern day family. It is alive with an abundance of biblical principles, modern day examples, and sound counsel. Its standards are high, but its message is down-to-earth. Walt is not afraid to surface some of today's tough problems plaguing the family and face them head-on.

Throughout the book there is a call to total dependence upon God which is demonstrated by a trust in the Holy Spirit, obedience to the Word of God, and the necessity of prayer—both with and for the family. Walt has done his homework in setting before us a book that gives us positive solutions to the problems that many families are grappling with today. I could only wish that I had had this book in our home when our three children were growing up.

Too often parents who fully realize the responsibility to make disciples among all nations forget that the process begins at home with their own children. With God-given conviction, Walt hammers this point home with great effectiveness.

I heartily recommend this book to all parents who are concerned about their children's character development, commitment to Christ, and their ability to communicate their faith to the world around them.

LeRoy Eims
Colorado Springs, Colorado

INTRODUCTION

Unless the Lord builds the house,
   its builders labor in vain.
Unless the Lord watches over the city,
   the watchmen stand guard in vain.
Sons are a heritage from the Lord,
   children a reward from Him.
Blessed is the man
   whose quiver is full of them.
                    (Psalm 127:1, 3, 5)

Conscientious Christian parents find themselves dependent upon God's gracious providence in the raising of their children. The 127th Psalm is a beautiful reflection about children being gifts from God and filling their parents' hearts with joy. But unless the Lord watches over the children and does the building necessary in their lives, the parents' efforts are in vain.

Writing a book on discipling children is a bit presumptuous of me, since it is ultimately the Lord who does the discipling. For this reason I hesitated putting on paper the contents of this book. My wife and I are very much learners in this whole process of raising children. I don't suppose it's possible to know the kind of job you have done with your children until you get a good look at your grandchildren. We are still several years away from having that experience.

I yielded to the temptation of verbalizing my thoughts on the discipling of children—bringing them to maturity in the Lord. I hope that the struggles and aspirations of this one parent might be helpful to others who want their children to make their chief end in life "to glorify God and enjoy Him forever."

In no sense is this meant to be a manual or the "last word" on discipling. Rather it should be viewed as a compilation of ideas and principles that are fundamental in helping children to maximize their potential for Jesus Christ. To the degree that these principles appear self-evident and obvious, I have succeeded. They are meant to serve as a reminder of the awesome but wonderful task with which all parents are blessed.

1

Defining the Task

His very presence demanded respect as the tall, distinguished black man stepped before the battery of microphones for an interview with the news media. He was in town at the invitation of some Christian businessmen to speak at the mayor's prayer breakfast.

It was remarkable that this controversial person was even in that predominately white southern town. In years past he had been a member of the California-based Black Panthers—a radical black movement. Indicted along with others for breaking the law, he had fled the country. He became a candidate for the grace of God when it began to dawn on him that his problems followed him, rather than staying behind in the United States.

Returning to his country, he began to orient his activities toward searching for God's will.

Bright lights warmed the room and beads of perspiration ran down his face as he fielded one question after another. A lady from the local television station asked him what it was that had launched him on a path of rebellion years earlier. He paused to reflect for a moment. Then he said the process began when he was a boy of nine and his father had left his mother for another woman. That experience taught him that he could trust no one—not even his own father.

This story, tragically, is not unique. Young people today are looking for stability. Four characteristics contribute to the lack of stability in their lives:

1. A lack of trust. We have taught our progeny that they cannot trust anyone. The establishment, government, and large corporations are all held suspect, if not in contempt. The government has made grandiose promises that it cannot fulfill. Some parents make pledges they never keep. Led to expect great things, young people are constantly disappointed.

2. A lack of commitment. This second characteristic contributes to the lack of trust. When things get tough, some people simply quit and move on to greener pastures. Disagreements erupt in a marriage, and instead of weathering the storm, men and women opt for divorce.

3. Antiauthoritarianism. "We will not have this man ruling over us," is the battle cry of the day. Students rebel against teachers, parents, and law enforcement. Men do not want to submit to authority. Women do not wish to submit to their husbands. Liberty without restraints has become the goal of many.

4. Narcissism. People are engaged in a froth of activity seeking their own fulfillment. Left in their wake are the neglected children screaming for someone to care, someone worthy of respect, someone they can trust.

Discipling Begins at Home

Discipling is the voguish cliché of the church today. Every respectable congregation has a discipling program. Large churches have ministers of discipling. For most, however, discipling is done at the price of neglecting those who need it most: our children!

Discipling must begin with our children if it is ever to affect the rest of our culture. Before we go looking for people to disciple, we should start with our own families. For a few short years God has entrusted our children to our care. Whether for good or bad, we will mark them for eternity.

An unknown author said it this way, "Scratch the green rind of a sapling, or wantonly twist it in the soil, and a scarred or crooked oak will tell of the act for centuries to come. So it is with the teaching of youth, which make impressions on the mind and heart that are to last forever."

In the Book of Proverbs, Solomon said, "Train up a child in the way he should go: and when he is old, he will not depart from it" (22:6, KJV). There is both a promise and a principle in these words. The promise stems from our faithfully following the principle. If, as parents, we properly invest in our children, we can make a permanent difference in their adult lives.

Biblical Discipleship

As we look at some of the ingredients that go into influencing our children toward godliness, it may prove helpful to pause for a moment and examine the word *disciple*. How do the biblical writers use the word? What does it mean to disciple our children?

First of all, a *disciple is not a pupil*. In the earliest uses of the word *disciple*, a distinction was made between the two. The relationship of the disciple with his mentor is different from that of the pupil with his teacher. The latter relationship is rational and professional while the former is grounded on fellowship. The pupil pays money to his teacher, and for this payment certain knowledge or skills are imparted. The basis of the mentor's relationship with the disciple is a desire to impart a philosophy of life. Financial remuneration is not a consideration.

When Paul wrote to Timothy about their relationship, he reminded Timothy that he sought not to impart facts as much as he was a lifestyle. Paul said:

> You, however, know all about my teaching, my way of
> life, my purpose, faith, patience, love, endurance, persecu-

tions, sufferings—what kinds of things happened to me in Antioch, Iconium and Lystra, the persecutions I endured. Yet the Lord rescued me from all of them. In fact, everyone who wants to live a godly life in Christ Jesus will be persecuted (2 Tim. 3:10-12).

They experienced a togetherness in the totality of life. As a disciple, Timothy's goal was not to learn, but rather to share in the life of his mentor. The layers of hierarchy were missing. He was not Paul's slave or servant, but a friend and co-laborer. An intimacy in their relationship made the process of Paul's discipling of Timothy very successful.

Second, *the discipler is always a link between God and the disciple.* This is clearly seen in the Old Testament. Although the word *disciple* or its equivalent is rare in the history and writings of Israel, the relationship did exist between men such as Moses and Joshua, Elijah and Elisha, and Eli and Samuel.

The Judeo-Christian religion is a religion of revelation. It was never the will or word of man that was communicated, but that of God. In most cases people were disciples of God. It was His will they sought. They belonged to Him. The prophets and other men of God never spoke on their own account. They sometimes defended their cause, but they never fought for their own persons. Their whole work was based on that commission given to them by God: "For the prophecy came not in old time by the will of man: but holy men of God spake as they were moved by the Holy Spirit" (2 Peter 1:21, KJV).

Consequently, there was no veneration of Old Testament characters. For example, the legacy of Moses was not bound up with the veneration of his person. Samuel and the prophets looked back to the time of Moses, never to Moses himself. Jeremiah wrote of what God did through Moses, but the emphasis was on the acts of God, not on Moses. Moses was not a hero (Jer. 2:1ff). He was simply the vehicle of God.

This same attitude is carried over into the New Testament. In a couple of instances *disciple* is used in the New Testament to refer to someone who is following another person. Paul referred to his own disciples who had helped him escape from Damascus: "Then the disciples took him [Saul] by night, and let him down by the wall in a basket" (Acts 9:25, KJV). And in the Gospel of John we are introduced to the disciples of John the Baptist:

> The next day John was there again with two of his disciples. When he saw Jesus passing by, he said, "Look, the Lamb of God!"
> When the two disciples heard him say this, they followed Jesus (John 1:35-37).

In both cases it was the clear intent of these men that their disciples ultimately would become disciples of Jesus Christ. Other than these two exceptions, the followers of Jesus had no followers themselves who were called disciples. John the Baptist best articulates the attitude of those seeking to influence others for Christ: "He [Jesus] must increase, but I must decrease" (John 3:30, KJV).

Third, *being a disciple is always voluntary.* As people related to Jesus in His public ministry, He never softened the impact of His message to solicit their allegiance. On one occasion the implications of His doctrine tested His disciples. Jesus had performed a number of miracles, and then had followed them up with the great discourse on the Bread of Life. The people loved having their physical needs met. The feeding of the masses reminded them of the manna provided by God in the Exodus. But referring to Himself as the Bread of Life was too much. John records the narrative as follows:

> On hearing it, many of His disciples said, "This is a hard teaching. Who can accept it?"
> Aware that His disciples were grumbling about this, Jesus said to them, "Does this offend you? What if you see the Son of Man ascend to where He was before! The Spirit gives life; the flesh counts for nothing. The words I have spoken to you are spirit and they are life. Yet there are

some of you who do not believe." For Jesus had known from the beginning which of them did not believe and who would betray Him. He went on to say, "This is why I told you that no one can come to Me unless the Father has enabled him."

From this time many of His disciples turned back and no longer followed Him.

"You do not want to leave too, do you?" Jesus asked the Twelve.

Simon Peter answered Him, "Lord, to whom shall we go? You have the words of eternal life. We believe and know that You are the Holy One of God."

Then Jesus replied, "Have I not chosen you, the Twelve? Yet one of you is a devil!" (He meant Judas, the son of Simon Iscariot, who, though one of the Twelve, was later to betray Him.) John 6:60-71

Simon Peter, speaking on behalf of the Twelve, rejected Jesus' offer to depart on the basis that they had no real option. He said, "Knowing what we know, there is no other place to go."

Discipleship is designed by God with our best interests in mind. We do God no favor by committing ourselves to Him. It is He who does us the favor by offering us discipleship. From the Saviour's perspective, it is the only way to squeeze the maximum out of life. In New Testament terms, failing to be a disciple is failing to lock in with the Creator in a program that has eternal significance.

In discipling our children, the initiative must remain with them. To force commitment upon them without the presence of an inner conviction causes our children to live a lie.

Fourth, *discipleship is commitment to the Person of Christ.* As we have already seen, the solder that welds the disciple and discipler together is not found in the content of the message as much as in the strength of the relationship. The allegiance of Jesus' disciples was to His Person more than to what He said.

This is confirmed by their conduct in the days between the Crucifixion and the Resurrection.

The depression experienced by the disciples after His death is attributed to what happened to His Person. Reflecting on the wisdom of His teachings gave them no comfort. The disciples felt they had lost Him, and being with Him had been the attraction.

When Jesus reconstructed the inner circle of disciples, it was again around His Person. They believed Him to be the Messiah and were commissioned with the task of witnessing to others—the focal point of that witness being that Jesus Christ is God. This is of paramount importance in understanding Christian discipleship. Any commitment that exists between the disciple and his mentor has the fact of Jesus' authority in mind. The one training has no authority over the disciple other than that of biblical imperatives.

To disciple a peer, you do not have the same God-given responsibility that you have in rearing your children. The parent discipling his child is confronted with the task of fulfilling his obligation as a parent, while at the same time teaching his child that his allegiance must finally be to Jesus Christ. In a certain sense you are wearing two hats. The goal, however, remains the same—commitment to the Person of Christ.

Fifth, *discipleship deals more with the inner quality of life than with outward performance.* As you read the four Gospels and note the requirements Jesus makes for being a disciple, you discover that these Gospels are largely speaking to what a person *is* more than to what *he does.*

> A new commandment I give you: Love one another. As I have loved you, so you must love one another. All men will know that you are My disciples if you love one another (John 13:34-35).

The expressions of love deal with outward performance, but love itself is an attitude. Most of the Ten Commandments address themselves to performance. Jesus summarized them with the word *love:*

> Love the Lord your God with all your heart and with all your soul and with all your mind. . . . Love your neighbor as yourself (Matt. 22:37, 39).

Love God (commandments 1-4) and love your neighbor (commandments 5-10). The reason for the summary is that God is more interested in the inner attitude of love than the outer expression of performance. You can have performance without love, but you cannot have love without performance. "Then Jesus said to those Jews which believed on Him, 'If you continue in My Word, then are you My disciples indeed'" (John 8:31, KJV). The words of Jesus were not at that time recorded so it's obvious He was not referring to the study of His Word. Application of the Master's teaching is central to discipleship. To continue in His Word is to take what He has said and put it into practice. This results in an action that is founded on an attitude of submission to what Jesus commands.

"This is to My Father's glory, that you bear much fruit, showing yourselves to be My disciples" (John 15:8). It is unclear whether Jesus meant by the word *fruit,* the fruit of the Spirit (Gal. 5:22-23), the fruit of evangelism, or both. In either case, the outward manifestation is the product of an inner quality. People respond to Christ as they see you manifest the fruit of the Spirit, namely Christlikeness in your daily conduct.

"In the same way, any of you who does not give up everything he has cannot be My disciple" (Luke 14:33). Here we have an example of outward actions being the indication of inner sincerity and commitment. If we really believe the claims of Christ, we will forsake all for Him. To forsake *all* for Jesus requires a right concept of what it means to surrender to His Lordship. It is ludicrous to imagine that one must stand literally naked and penniless to qualify as a disciple. As important as the *doing* is, it must be the fruit of *being.*

The word *disciple* is mentioned about 250 times in the

Gospels and the Book of Acts. With the few exceptions mentioned above, the term denotes those people who have attached themselves to Jesus as their Master. *Disciple* never refers to what one person does with another person.

As a parent I do not convert my child to Christ. From first to last, it is the work of the Holy Spirit. I may be privileged to function as midwife in the new birth process, but that is all. So also in discipling, I will guide and influence my children, and that responsibility alone is awesome. But if I want my child to be a disciple of Jesus Christ, it is He who must give form and content to the relationship.

Motivating Your Children

Have you ever been frustrated by the fact that something which is so clear and obvious to you seems to elude others? Have you ever wished that you could reach inside a person and change his sense of values? Have you ever felt like taking someone by the shoulders and saying, "Why can't you see it?" If you are like most people, you have. That person may well have been your child. As a matter of fact, what you wanted him to see might have been so obvious to you that you may have suspected he did not want to see it. His blindness, you felt, was rooted in rebellion!

All of us have had such frustrating experiences. The truth is, a person cannot reach inside of another person and change his perception. You can force a person to do something. You can even make him sorry that he did not do it. But you cannot convince a person against his will.

How then do you motivate your children in directions that they appear to resist? The Holy Spirit, God's Word, and the example of committed Christians are crucial in motivating your children to follow Christ.

The Holy Spirit. It is the Spirit of God who reaches inside of a person and motivates him to action. He is able to change this person's sense of values and perspective. You have seen it in your own life. Many of the ideas and convictions you held 10 years ago have been modified. So also 10 years from now you will see things slightly different than you do today. This is part of the process of sanctification.

Our children are the same. They too must be shaped by the Holy Spirit. Our responsibility as parents in this regard is prayer. Prayer does change people. As we plead the cause of our children before the throne of grace, the Holy Spirit does His work in their hearts. The importance of prayer permeates all of what is being said in this book.

The Word of God. The writer to the Hebrews said:

> For the word of God is quick, and powerful, and sharper than any two-edged sword, piercing even to the dividing asunder of soul and spirit, and of the joints and marrow, and is a discerner of the thoughts and intents of the heart (Heb. 4:12, KJV).

Exposure to the Scriptures has a profound impact on a person. As you counsel your child, constantly refer to the Bible. When correcting your child, refer him back to the Scriptures. Ask, "What does God say?" Help him to see, through the Word, the greatness of God and the importance of giving his life in exchange for that which is eternal. Challenge him to get into the Word—to study, memorize, and read it. Be careful not to make it a condition of your acceptance. Rather, emphasize the importance of a life saturated in the Scriptures.

Example. Albert Schweitzer once said, "Example is not *a* way to teach; it is the *only* way to teach." You may want to modify that statement, but the importance of example cannot be overlooked. In chapter 3 we will explore the important role Mom and Dad play in motivating children to godliness. But Mom and Dad are not the only examples.

There are a multitude of people God will bring into your children's lives which will help shape them into Christ's image. Just as in the physical realm you are not responsible for meeting all your children's needs, but in seeing that they are met; so also in the spiritual. For example, if your son breaks his arm, you don't try to set it, but you take him to an orthopedic surgeon. If your daughter needs braces on her teeth, you take her to an orthodontist. You would be negligent only if you don't see to it that these important matters are done.

The analogy carries over into the spiritual realm as well. Our churches, missionaries that come through our homes, and evangelical agencies like Young Life and Youth for Christ are all helpful in the task of motivating and training our children to walk in a manner that is worthy of the Lord. As parents we must not be threatened by them, nor become overly dependent upon them. It is a team effort with us functioning as coaches.

God must work in our children "to will and to act according to His good purpose" (Phil. 2:13). We as parents function as catalysts in a process that is His. It is an important function, but also a limited one.

2

It's a Sin to Bore Kids with the Gospel

Jim Rayburn was a man who loved kids. He was a man who also loved Christ. *How do you get kids to fall in love with Christ?* This question burned in Jim's soul and gave birth to the Young Life Campaign.

It was Jim's observation that most kids are not turned off with Christianity, but with a caricature of it. Their perception of it is that the rigid rules and regulations rob life of fun and fulfillment. Christianity is a religion of repression, forcing people to do what they don't want to do. It is a sober religion where to laugh is sacrilege.

Jesus said, "I am come that they might have life, and that they might have it more abundantly" (John 10:10b, KJV). He did not come to take life, but to impart it. It is the world that doesn't know how to live. Christianity teaches people how to get the maximum out of life. Any representation of Christianity to the contrary is a travesty of the truth. It is sin!

The parent who wants to disciple his child must come to grips with this. Christianity is not boring, nor is it dead. It is exciting and alive. Often when our children become turned off with the Gospel, we blame it on their lack of commitment. However, before we arrive at so glib a conclusion, we should look at our presentation of the Gospel. I must confess that much of what I see in evangelical Christianity is unimaginative and uninteresting. It *is* downright boring.

You Are the Pacesetter

Children take their cues from us as their parents. By and large, they mirror our attitudes. If we are positive and excited about Christ and our walk with Him, they will be also. If they sense that we are glad to have them around and that we love our roles as parents, they will respond in like manner.

One set of parents I know constantly talked about the problems they had with their children. First it was the terrible twos. Then it was the traumatic threes. From there it went to the frantic fours, and on up. By the time the children were in their teens, to hear them talk, these parents were raising a household of monsters. Tragically, the children were simply living up to their parents' expectations. Mom and Dad expected them to be terrors and terrors they were.

I was listening to a mother talk one day and learned that she was giving her young son tranquilizers. He was an excited, happy-go-lucky little guy. To her, he was Dennis the Menace. Instead of praying over creative ways of channeling all that energy, she drugged him.

Another husband and wife I know quite well talk in glowing terms about the day when their children will be grown and on their own. Then the parents can begin to live their own lives. They are communicating to their children that they are keeping Mom and Dad from doing what they really want to do. How unwanted can children feel?

These are all Christian parents raising their children in Christian homes. No wonder young people are staying away from church in droves!

Where is the good news of the Gospel in their attitudes? Where is the abundant life Jesus promised to bring? If we are not communicating this to our children, then we are failing in our sacred trust and commitment.

Learn to enjoy your children. Become excited about their interests. Let them know there is nothing in the world you would rather do than be their parents. Follow Paul's advice to the Romans and rejoice with them when they rejoice and weep with them when they weep. (See Rom. 12:15.)

Sage Advice for the Learner

One of the richest sources of creative ideas on how to disciple children is from other Christian parents who are doing a superb job with their children. Here is a collection of observations my wife and I have made through the years that may help you too:

Think positively. Bill and Jan have six children. They are all grown now and a healthier brood would be hard to find. All six of them are excited and positive in their commitments to Christ. They love people and carry with them that air of graciousness that is so infectious.

I asked Bill one day what his secret was. From a human perspective, how did he and Jan do it? He said that in their family they had very few rules. They concentrated on the positive rather than on the negative. A passage they studied over and over again in their family unit was Deuteronomy 6:4-5:

> Hear, O Israel: The Lord our God is one Lord: And thou shalt love the Lord thy God with all thine heart, and with all thy soul, and with all thy might (KJV).

As a family, they spent hours talking about these verses and asking: "What does it mean to love God? How should that be reflected in our lifestyle?" Bill and Jan were convinced that if their family loved God the way He ought to be loved, everything else would fall into place. This is what Martin Luther had in mind when he said, "Love God and do as you please." If you love God, what you please will be what He pleases.

Because Bill and Jan majored in the positive with their children, their children were positive in their commitments to Christ.

Avoid snap decisions. Charles and Judy have four children. Similar to Bill and Jan's family, theirs is grown, out of the nest, and they all love the Lord. Their daughter is a vivacious person who comes up with a new idea every minute. Some of her ideas are good and some are not so good, but all of them are enthusiastically presented and carry a tone of urgency. Some of her ideas can be endorsed by Charles and Judy and some cannot. Most of them don't require a quick decision. Rather than immediately responding to their daughter with a vote of approval or disapproval, they receive her ideas positively and tell her they will talk them over and pray about them.

If, after discussing her ideas, they feel they have to say no, enough time has lapsed so that she is no longer emotionally involved. Often, if a particular idea is a poor one, she herself has second thoughts by the time a verdict is given.

Because Charles and Judy didn't make snap decisions concerning their children's requests, they avoided negative reactions.

Show your children how. Sam and Molly have younger children. One day Sam and I were spending time together praying for our families and sharing ideas. Here is a lesson the Lord taught him.

In past weeks he had found he was constantly correcting his son. The dishes weren't done properly, he did a poor job washing the automobile, or the windows had smears on them when he finished cleaning them. As Sam prayed over this, it dawned on him it was easier to criticize his son for what was wrong than to take time to show him why and how to do it properly. The reason his son did a poor job cleaning the car was because Sam had never taken the time to show him the right way to do it. He wasn't slothful or lazy; rather, he was untaught.

Sam learned to show his child how and why it was important to do it right rather than telling him that he was doing it wrong.

Learn from your children. Fred and Lois are learners. Every day is a school day. It doesn't matter who they're with or what is being discussed, you sense their eagerness to learn. When one of their children arrives home with a fresh idea, Mom and Dad become as excited as if he or she were Ponce de León discovering the fountain of life.

Fred is forever taking notes. He frequently carries a pad of paper for that purpose. Not that he is uneducated—quite the opposite. It's just that he has never graduated from the school of life. This is extremely motivating to their four children. Each one can say, "Not only are Mom and Dad interested in what I am doing, they are actually learning from me."

We also know parents who communicate the opposite principle. You can't teach them anything. If one of their children comes home with a new idea or fact, the response is always the same. "We're glad to see *you* have discovered that at last."

Fred and Lois knew that if they were willing to learn from their children, their children would be willing to learn from them.

Concentrate on your children's strengths. Bob and Mary have four boys. They are all different. They come in different sizes, shapes, and looks. They have different gifts, temperaments, and interests. Bob and Mary made it their job to discover the strengths in each of their children and then they concentrated on these strengths. They did this in academics, athletics, and the arts. What was one child's strength was another child's weakness. Rather than trying to make the children conform to a single pattern, Bob and Mary emphasized their children's individual strengths in positive ways.

Quite often a strength has a corresponding weakness and a weakness has a corresponding strength. Moses was the meekest man on the earth; yet a fit of anger kept him from the Promised Land. Peter was fiercely loyal to Christ, even willing to take up his sword in His defense. But it was Peter who denied Christ.

Many parents feel that if they concentrate on their children's weaknesses, their strengths will take care of themselves. Actually, the opposite is true. To focus on weaknesses rather than strengths is to produce mediocrity in children. This is not to suggest that weaknesses should be ignored; rather we should not lay stress upon them.

Whether it was in their character or their gifts and abilities, Bob and Mary concentrated on their children's strengths rather than their weaknesses.

Take time with your children. Pete and Millie have a couple of inquisitive teenagers. They're constantly looking for new adventures. The children aren't bad, they just don't want to miss anything life has to offer. Consequently, they sometimes veer off course.

Rather than lecture their son and daughter on model behavior, Pete and his wife buy up their teenagers' time. They set aside weekends to do special things with either or both of them before the problem gets out of hand. Pete might take off from work early and meet his daughter after school to go shopping and then take her out to dinner. He stays close to her until she has passed through her crisis and then he resumes his normal activities.

Sometimes this means cutting back on evening socials, Bible studies, or other activities. Once it meant that Pete had to take part of his vacation early. All of this was done without his teenager knowing what was happening. There were no sermons and no lectures.

When their teenager was in trouble, Pete and Millie bought up his time, and in the process loved him back to responsible behavior.

Invest in memories. Tom and Ruth have very few valuable things. But they and their family have a treasure house full of wonderful memories. Early in their marriage they decided they would invest in memories rather than things. Things wear out—memories last a lifetime.

They have consistently invested their limited resources in activities which build precious memories. One year they all went to Europe, bought a secondhand Volkswagen camper, and toured the great cities. On another occasion the whole family visited missionary friends in a remote area of Mexico and spent their vacation on a building project.

The activities are always chosen in family concert as each member brings to the group his or her ideas. The building of memories begins with months of preparation and lingers long afterward as they look at their pictures and share their experiences.

Special occasions are important for this family. Each child's birthday is a special event. Christmas is a season rather than a day. Discipleship has more to do with what the family is than what the family does. It is during these times of togetherness that the foundations of discipleship are constantly being built.

All through the Bible, God admonishes His people to remember. Remembering what God has done for us in the past is essential for proper living in the future. This is also true in the lives of our children. The memories they have of their childhood days will help determine the kinds of disciples they become as adults.

To Tom and Ruth, memories were more important than things.

Let them develop convictions. Ralph and Joan have a teenage daughter who questions everything. The most important word in Debbie's vocabulary is *why*. Her questioning is so persistent, it is sometimes difficult to determine if her questions are honest ones.

One day Debbie announced to her parents that she was tired of going to church. The whole experience, she thought, was a bore. My wife and I were fascinated as we observed Ralph and Joan handle this one. Rather than forcing their daughter to join them on Sunday, they permitted her to stay home. As Ralph and I talked about it, he explained that he could force Debbie to go to church with him, but that would only postpone the problem. He would rather have his daughter work through her own convictions while still under his roof than wait until she moved out on her own when his influence would be minimal.

At that point in her life, Debbie felt her parents were legalistic in their commitment to Christ. The difference between legalism and discipline is difficult for many people to sort out. Legalism is doing the right thing for the wrong reason. Discipline is doing the right thing for the right reason. Ralph and Joan were trying to help their daughter move from legalism to a lifestyle of discipline. This could only be done by allowing her an opportunity to develop her own convictions.

Ralph and Joan didn't feel threatened by Debbie's questioning, but rather they gave her an opportunity to formulate her own convictions.

Don't let your career be a tyrant. Ted and Debbie have a family of five. For years they were successfully involved in the retail business. As they evaluated the needs of their growing children, they concluded that exposure to another culture would be beneficial in discipling their children. They sold their business and moved to Latin America.

It was a positive time for the whole family as they set aside the creature comforts of the United States for the exposure to a less developed country. The needs of the children took precedence over the parents' careers and aspirations.

A certain amount of risk is involved in making this kind of decision. The family is uprooted. Also, financial loss, and lack of access to quality education and medicine are felt. Yet Ted and Debbie made their decision on the basis of the inner person and how it could best be developed rather than majoring in creature comforts.

The development of their children was more important to Ted and Debbie than the development of their careers.

It's an Adventure

Listening, giving, sharing—these are the ingredients that go into the discipling process. The result is a life of adventure. It is the only way we can glean from life all that God intended. If we communicate any less to our children either by our attitudes or by our lifestyle, we prostitute the Gospel and do them a terrible wrong.

This is what Jim Rayburn had in mind when he said, "It is a sin to bore kids with the Gospel."

3
Parents Set the Example

On parent knees, a naked newborn child,
Weeping thou sat'st, when all around thee smil'd;
So live, that, sinking in thy last long sleep,
Calm thou may'st smile, while all around thee weep.

In these poetic lines, Sir William Jones captured the challenge of parenthood. The happy effort mingled with tears that parents put into rearing their children will reap the dividends of a job well done. As parents slip into the presence of God, it will be the children who weep as they comtemplate the loss of those who have made so significant a contribution to their lives.

The fact that each child has a mother and dad is no accident. A team effort is required in raising children. Each child needs two parents who are modeling the dynamics of well-rounded lives. It is as the child observes Mom and Dad relating to one another, for example, that he learns how to properly relate to his spouse later. Someone once said, "Parents who wish to train their children in the way they should go, must go in the way in which they would have their children go."

This is a theme repeatedly emphasized in the Bible and is of such importance that we do well to investigate it.

The Husband-Wife Relationship

There are several passages in Scripture that deal dynamically with this subject; for instance 1 Peter 3:1-6. The verses deal with the role of a wife. Peter speaks of a godly wife's behavior, dress, and example:

> Wives, in the same way be submissive to your husbands so that, if any of them do not believe the Word, they may be won over without talk by the behavior of their wives, when they see the purity and reverence [fear] of your lives. Your beauty should not come from outward adornment, such as braided hair and the wearing of gold jewelry and fine clothes. Instead, it should be that of your inner self, the unfading beauty of a gentle and quiet spirit, which is of great worth in God's sight. For this is the way the holy women of the past who put their hope in God used to make themselves beautiful. They were submissive to their own husbands, like Sarah, who obeyed Abraham and called him her master. You are her daughters if you do what is right and do not give way to fear.

Her behavior (1 Peter 3:1-2). Three words characterize the behavior of a wife as outlined by Peter. The first is *submission*. It is the idea of "falling into step with," "under the authority of," or "picking up the same cadence." It is the responsibility of the wife to fall into step with the husband, not vice versa.

All people are under authority. Children are in submission to their parents. Wives are in submission to their husbands. This does not mean, however, that the wives cannot be involved in business, government, and other experiences. If their husbands are in agreement, and if both husband and wife feel it is not to the neglect of their children, there is no biblical injunction against wives pursuing careers of their own.

Note what Peter *does not* say, and what he *does* say. He does not say that a wife is to submit to her husband because he is right, or worthy, or because he loves her the way she ought to be loved but only because he is her husband. But there are some biblical absolutes, and if she were asked to break one of the express moral laws of God, then she must respectfully disobey her husband in order to obey God. For the average wife, this will rarely happen. Her spirit of submission will cause her husband to dislike confrontation with her. Her prayers likewise can do much to change matters. Peter assumes she may be married to a non-Christian, but she is still to be in submission to him, unless in so doing she opposes God.

Note also what Peter does say. "Wives, in the same way be submissive to your husbands" (1 Peter 3:1). The words *in the same way* suggest a prior example. As we look back into 1 Peter 2, we find the example in Jesus Christ. The heart of the example is found in verses 20-23:

> But how is it to your credit if you receive a beating for doing wrong and endure it? But if you suffer for doing good and you endure it, this is commendable before God. To this you were called, because Christ suffered for you, leaving you an example, that you should follow in His steps. "He committed no sin, and no deceit was found in His mouth." When they hurled their insults at Him, He did not retaliate; when He suffered, He made no threats. Instead, He entrusted Himself to Him who judges justly.

A wife's example of submission is her Saviour. The issue is not whether she is right or wrong—any more than that was the issue of Jesus' example of suffering in chapter 2. Rather, the issue is submission to God-ordained authority.

The second key word in these verses is *purity* (v. 2). It means, "that which awakens religious awe." A wife should conduct herself in a pure and holy way, saving herself only for her husband.

My daughter and I were eating out one evening, and enjoying a long chat. The subject of purity and holiness came up. Just then an attractive, scantily-clad, young lady walked into the room. I suggested that my daughter notice the eyes of the men as they watched this young lady walk by.

"Oh, Daddy," she said, embarrassed. "I didn't know that that is how men look at women."

The Christlike wife conducts herself in a manner that awakens religious awe in men rather than impure desires. This is what is modeled before her watching children.

The third key word in these first two verses is *reverence* (v. 2). Reverence is a fear based on love. It carries the idea of respect. This is the behavior of the godly wife.

Her dress (1 Peter 3:3-4). Peter suggests what a wife's adorning is not (v. 3). It is not a preoccupation with outward appearance. An unhealthy preoccupation with her looks usually is an indication that she is unsure of herself. There is balance here—between not looking shabby and unkempt on the one hand, and making her appearance the most important thing on the other. Her children will mirror the degree to which she is able to maintain this balance.

A wife's real adorning is her inner person—a gentle and quiet spirit (v. 4). Quiet does not mean silent. The wife is not called upon to be a docile, unresponsive wallflower. The quiet spirit means she is not argumentative, combative, and domineering. When a wife nags her husband, either he gives in, resents it, and begins to look elsewhere for understanding and fulfillment, or he becomes stubborn and they constantly fight with one another.

Her example (1 Peter 3:5-6). We all need prototypes. What are they supposed to look like? Peter suggests that the Old Testament women of God are Christian wives' prototypes; the holy women of old in general and Sarah in particular. A couple of thoughts on these verses:

1. Christian wives' examples in verses 5-6 are all human and thus attainable. They were women who fought the same temptations and inner struggles as women today. Paul reminds us that we do not face unique temptations (see 1 Cor. 10:13). Sarah had to honor Abraham as master. And, it must have been

hard sometimes for Sarah to submit to her husband. For example, on two occasions he tried to pass her off as his sister for fear of harm coming to him.

2. There are no cultural considerations in these verses. Peter writes to people scattered throughout a variety of cultures in the Roman Empire. For illustration he goes back 2,000 years to a woman living in a different culture and time. In this he is suggesting that the biblical role of the wife is transcultural. Consistently, the Bible's writers root their arguments regarding women, not in culture, but by creation; namely, this is the way God has made the sexes and these are their respective roles.

A Christlike husband:

Husbands, in the same way be considerate as you live with your wives, and treat them with respect as the weaker partner and as heirs with you of the gracious gift of life, so that nothing will hinder your prayers (1 Peter 3:7).

Here in verse 7, we see two commands and a condition for Christian husbands:

Command 1: Knowledge. When Peter says husbands are to dwell with their wives according to knowlege, he is referring to what the Bible says. Husbands are to treat their wives with the knowledge revealed in the Scriptures. This is in contrast to how the world treats women.

Historically, the emancipation and liberation given to women is the product of the Christian teaching of the worth of an individual. This can be clearly seen in cultures outside the Judeo-Christian tradition. For example, in India prior to the British presence, widows of Hindus were burned alive on the biers of their dead husbands. In many of the North American Indian tribes, the widows were left to fend for themselves, resulting in their deaths by starvation and exposure.

A Christian husband is to be different. He is not to treat his wife as a chattel. He is to honor and cherish her as one created in the image of God—as God's own daughter.

Command 2: Heirs. The wife is joint-heir with the husband in *all* that God offers His children. In every sense of the word, she is his spiritual equal. The wife is in submission to her husband, but this does not mean that he is better than she; any more than a general is better than a private or an employer than an employee, or God the Father than God the Son.

All people are to be under authority by God's standard. The husband is under the authority of Christ, the government, the elders of his church, and his employer. Submission is a key word in Peter's epistle. First Peter 2:13-16 is an example of this:

> Submit yourselves for the Lord's sake to every authority instituted among men: whether to the king, as the supreme authority, or to governors, who are sent by him to punish those who do wrong and to commend those who do right. For it is God's will that by doing good you should silence the ignorant talk of foolish men. Live as free men, but do not use your freedom as a cover-up for evil; live as servants of God.

People who rebel against all authority are slaves to anarchy. Both parents are to be submissive to God-given authority. For the wife, this is her husband. But remember, says Peter, she is heir with her husband of the grace of life.

Condition: Prayers will not be hindered. These words are written to the husband. If he fails to treat his wife with the proper knowledge and respect—if he fails to regard her as an equal heir—then God will not hear his prayers.

Note how Peter emphasizes this point: "For the eyes of the Lord are over the righteous, and His ears are open unto their prayers; but the face of the Lord is against them that do evil" (1 Peter 3:12, KJV). Because the wife is under the authority of her husband, "as the weaker partner," the Lord takes a special interest in seeing that her needs are met.

Parental Patterns

As we parents relate to one another, a certain attitude is caught by our children. What we are communicates far more than what we teach. How my son someday relates to his wife will be a reflection of how I relate to my wife.

Paul, in his letter to the church at Ephesus, goes to great lengths in teaching families how to relate to one another. He begins his teaching on various roles with the words: "Submit to one another out of reverence for Christ" (Eph. 5:21). It is not just the wife who is to be in submission, nor just the children. Each of us is to assume a posture of submission to one another. It is precisely this attitude of humility and sensitivity to the desires of others that creates an environment that communicates to our children what discipleship is all about.

Care must be taken to preach to ourselves our own sermons and not major in preaching to others. As a husband I am to preach to myself, "Love your wife as Christ loved the church" rather than, "Wife, be submissive to me." As a father I must focus on not provoking my children to wrath rather than on their obeying my every word. This doesn't negate obedience to parents. But by my attitude, I convey a spirit of cooperation and mutual submission that makes it easier for my children to be obedient.

Some parents once said to me, "We argue in front of our children so they can know how to argue with their spouses someday and learn how to reconcile their differences." Such thinking is not likely to produce the desired results. It is like saying that our children learn what not to do through our bad examples. The Bible always calls upon us to perform at our highest level. We teach our children godliness by responding to circumstances in a godly way. We may lose our tempers and raise our voices with one another, we may argue and fight with one another, but we must never try to excuse it as being natural or human or desirable. Call it for what it is—sin. God does not want our children to be natural. He wants them to be supernatural. This is what the fruit of the Spirit is about in Galatians 5:22-23.

Responding to Our Children
How we parents respond to one another is critically important

in influencing children. Important also is how we relate to our children. To stimulate our thinking in this area, here are some questions we can ask ourselves:

1. Do we understand that our children's concept of God is influenced by us? Throughout the Bible, family language is used in transmitting God's relationship to His people. God is our Father. We are His children. Jesus is God's Son. The church is the bride of Christ, and so on. We are to act with our children the way God acts with us. Conversely, our children are led to believe that how we relate to them is how God relates to His children.

2. We love our children, but do we enjoy them? I don't believe I've ever met a parent who didn't profess to love his children. Many parents, however, don't really enjoy them. They communicate the need to "get away from the kids for awhile." When they have dinner with friends, the children are excluded if possible. Rather than taking an active interest in what their children are doing, they are either too busy or become annoyed with their children's immature ways. Not infrequently I hear parents say, "We can't wait until the kids are grown and gone so we can be on our own. Then we can start doing some of the things we've always wanted to do." This attitude speaks volumes to their children—all of it wrong. We touched on this in an earlier chapter, but this selfish attitude is so prevalent and so counterproductive to the discipling process, it needs underlining once again. The folly of it is seen by simply asking ourselves if we would like God to relate to us in this same manner.

3. As our children mature, are we willing to relate to them as peers? For many parents this is one of the most difficult hurdles to jump. One of the healthiest examples of this I've ever seen is a father-son relationship in Michigan. The son, now in his 20s, is an equal in the eyes of his father. His dad treats him like a peer, asks his counsel on matters, leans on his son's expertise, and confides in him. He allows his son to take the same risks that he took when he was in his 20s. Somewhere along the line, the umbilical cord was cut and the boy became his own man before God—and his father.

4. Is our love and acceptance of our children unconditional? The idea of unconditional love is unique to the Bible. It is based on the fact that God's commitment to His people is unconditional. There will be times when we disappoint our Lord, but we will never surprise Him. He knows us from beginning to end. His love is not based on our performance or godliness. It is based solely on the finished work of Christ.

The non-Christian knows of love. But his love is based on reciprocity. If his love is returned and if his expectations are met, then his love is unthreatened. If, however, his love is unrequited, it is rescinded. This is illustrated by the boy who was the apple of his father's eye. When the boy entered young adulthood and embraced a lifestyle unacceptable to his dad, he became *persona non grata* in the family unit.

Our love and acceptance of our family must be a mirror of God's love. As parents we are vulnerable. We can be wounded by our children. But this is never an excuse for withdrawing our love. Our children may do many things that we cannot condone. But our acceptance of them is unconditional and irrevocable.

Discipling our children is more than dogma and programs. Most importantly, it is a quality of life absorbed by our children from us who are parents. The example we set makes or breaks everything else we do. If there is something attractive about the way we live, then our children will become infected with a desire to emulate it. We are the principle influences in the lives of these would-be disciples of Jesus Christ. This is the challenge of Christian parenthood.

4

God's Value System

Jesus was in the last year of His public ministry. The opposition was growing as He set His face toward Jerusalem and the cross. It was an intense time of training for the disciples as Jesus prepared them for His departure.

A major source of conflict with the Pharisees was Jesus' constant identification with the publicans and sinners. Righteous people had no dealings with this segment of society. And yet it was to this group of people that the Saviour gravitated.

Their conflicting philosophies of life were far from superficial. From Jesus' perspective people were important—of *eternal* value. To drive this home, Luke records a trilogy of parables, all dealing with our Lord's objective. (See Luke 15.) The third in a series (Luke 15:11-32) is the famous Parable of the Prodigal Son. Like the father in the story, our heavenly Father is eager for us to come to Him and enjoy His care instead of the pleasures of the world. The mission of Jesus was to mediate that restoration.

Jesus felt that the lesson must be indelibly etched on the minds of His Twelve Apostles. In God's economy *people* are of supreme worth. To give your life in exchange for anything else is an investment in trivia.

The Use of Riches

Thus Jesus followed through with still another parable—that of the Unjust Steward. Like the parables before, our Lord was teaching the disciples the need for a proper value system. The parables of the Lost Sheep (Luke 15:3-7), the Lost Coin (Luke 15:8-10), and the Lost Son (Luke 15:11-32), all highlight the ministry of the Saviour and why He invested Himself in people. The Parable of the Unjust Steward is a lesson in contrasts. "The people of this world are more shrewd in dealing with their own kind than are the people of light" (Luke 16:8)—in that they give their lives for what they *think to be most important,* namely, riches. In contrast, the "people of light" exchange their lives for that which they *know to be the least important,* that is, riches. Look more closely at the parable as it unfolds in Luke 16:1-9:

Jesus told His disciples: "There was a rich man whose manager was accused of wasting his possessions. So he called him in and asked him, 'What is this I hear about you? Give an account of your management, because you cannot be manager any longer.'

"The manager said to himself, 'What shall I do now? My master is taking away my job. I'm not strong enough to dig, and I'm ashamed to beg—I know what I'll do so that, when I lose my job here, people will welcome me into their houses.'

"So he called in each one of his master's debtors. He asked the first, 'How much do you owe my master?'

" 'Eight hundred gallons of olive oil,' he replied.

"The manager told him, 'Take your bill, sit down quickly, and make it four hundred.'

"Then he asked the second, 'And how much do you owe?'

" 'A thousand bushels of wheat,' he replied.

"He told him, 'Take your bill and make it eight hundred.'

"The master commended the dishonest manager because he had acted shrewdly. For the people of this world are more shrewd in dealing with their own kind than are the people of light. I tell you, use worldly wealth to gain friends for yourselves, so that when it is gone, you will be welcomed into eternal dwellings."

This story is about a wealthy man who was probably in the wholesale business. He dealt in large quantities of oil and wheat. His steward, probably the foreman or manager, was accused of waste. It wasn't theft, but the misappropriation of his employer's resources that caught up with him.

Realizing that his days were numbered, the steward quickly and privately called in the debtors and settled for a fraction of the bill. The collected moneys were no doubt turned over to the employer. What the steward was doing was winning the debtors to himself instead of to the master. Then, when he was unemployed, he could collect on the favors shown. Not only was the employer impressed with his shrewdness; Jesus was also.

Lest our moral sensibilities become offended, let's unravel the teachings of this parable. In many ways we can compare the unjust steward to a believer:

- He was a steward—and so is a believer.
- He was entrusted with valuables—and so is a believer.
- The valuables were "unrighteous mammon" (riches)— and so are the believer's valuables.
- He made friends by using the riches—a believer can do the same.
- He had to give an account to his master—the believer will have to do likewise.
- He came to an end—and so will the believer.

It is at this point that the parable takes a different turn:

- The steward gave his life to riches—the believer gives his life to God.

- The steward was motivated by unrighteousness—the believer is motivated by righteousness.

As the steward found his home and income gone, he had to prepare for another home. The believer must also prepare for the day when he will leave this life.

But why does Jesus use the example of an *unrighteous* steward? In pondering this question, ask yourself, "What is the most important thing to the non-Christian?" If you define mammon as money and the things that money can buy, the answer is obviously *money*.

For one born of the Spirit, what *should* be the most important thing? The answer is obviously God and that which He declares to be important, namely *people*. Jesus gave up His life in exchange for people.

It is at this point that the unbeliever is often wiser than the children of light. The unbeliever *thinks* he is giving his life in exchange for that which is the *most* significant when he gives it for riches. But when the believer gives his life for riches, he *knows* he is giving it for that which is *least* significant, and in the process he is showing the world and his family a faulty value system.

With piercing rhetoric Jesus drives home the application for believers: Use your riches to your advantage. Use your riches for that which is eternal rather than for that which is temporal, and for people instead of for that which someday will perish. As Christians you are not in the land of the living moving toward the land of the dying. Rather, you are in the land of the dying moving toward the land of the living. Therefore, live like it. Make sure your value system is a reflection of this fact.

The Value of Riches

Jesus told His disciples, "Whoever can be trusted with very little can also be trusted with much, and whoever is dishonest with very little will also be dishonest with much.

So if you have not been trustworthy in handling worldly wealth, who will trust you with true riches? And if you have not been trustworthy with someone else's property, who will give you property of your own?" (Luke 16:10-12)

As we have already seen, the way we use our resources is an indication of our perspective on life. The way we handle riches is a mirror of our attitudes and abilities which will reflect in how we handle spiritual rewards. These same attitudes will also be reflected in the lives of our children. If there is any doubt in our minds where we stand on this issue, we can simply ask our children what they have observed to be the most important things in our lives.

A True Value System

Jesus suggests two ways of determining your true value system:

1. The things you talk about (Matt. 12:34b): "For out of the overflow of the heart the mouth speaks."

2. Where your money is invested (Luke 12:34): "For where your treasure is, there your heart will be also."

This second indicator in Luke 12 is the climax of another parable that Jesus told.

> And He told them this parable: "The ground of a certain rich man produced a good crop. He thought to himself, 'What shall I do? I have no place to store my crops.'
>
> "Then he said, 'This is what I'll do. I will tear down my barns and build bigger ones, and there I will store all my grain and my goods. And I'll say to myself, "You have plenty of good things laid up for many years. Take life easy; eat, drink, and be merry."'
>
> "But God said to him, 'You fool! This very night your life will be demanded from you. Then who will get what you have prepared for yourself?'
>
> "This is how it will be with anyone who stores up things for himself but is not rich toward God" (Luke 12:16-21).

This is a proper indictment for all who invest their lives in things. Again and again the Bible cautions us to invest in that which makes us rich toward God.

Investing our time *for* our children is different than investing our time *in* our children. Many parents spend the bulk of their energies acquiring things and justifying it with, "I am doing it for my family." Our families don't need material things half as badly as they need our companionship. If this sounds radical and somewhat hard, it is because we have allowed ourselves to drift into conformity with our society's way of thinking.

Jesus told His disciples: "Whoever can be trusted with very little can also be trusted with much, and whoever is dishonest with very little will also be dishonest with much" (Luke 16:10-12). Our natural response is to think otherwise: *Little things aren't important, but if given a truly significant task, then I would produce.* Not so, says Jesus. Even corporate life substantiates His claim. A neophyte joining a bank is not immediately made president. He must prove himself faithful in menial tasks before he can expect advancement.

If we major in accumulating riches to the neglect of discipling our children, the watching world may think we are successful, but these riches will not be acclaimed as successful when we face our Lord in eternity.

Resisting the Deceptive Power of Money

"No servant can serve two masters. Either he will hate the one and love the other, or he will be devoted to the one and despise the other. You cannot serve both God and Money" (Luke 16:13).

No man can serve two masters *equally*. Many try to make God and money equal in their lives. But they always fail, says Jesus. They always lose. They can count on losing whenever they allow their hearts to become ensnared with money and the things money can buy, and God is relegated to a place of secondary importance. This is the reason believers need to resist money's deceptive power.

Mike is a man committed to Christ. He had some investments in the stock market, but found that they consumed his thought life. If he was not preoccupied with the gyrations of the market, he was dreaming of how he would spend his capital gains. Morning and night he looked at the stock report to see how his investments were doing. He finally got out of the market.

It was not that the stock market was wrong. There is nothing unbiblical about owning stock. What was wrong was Mike's preoccupation with it. He could not leave it alone. No one told him he had to get out. In his own heart he felt he had to in order to serve only one Master.

The parable points to a choice: what the world judges to be important versus what God judges to be important. We cannot have it both ways. If we elect money to be the most important, we choose a wrong value system for ourselves and teach our children the same.

The Process and the Product

As we seek to impart a proper value system to our children, we can verbalize what we know to be true, but the process requires our living up to our convictions, if it is to mean anything to our children. The process has a tendency to work something like this:

- The first generation is willing to die for their ideas of a proper value system.
- The second generation is willing to believe these ideas, if they are that important to Mom and Dad.
- The third generation questions the ideas.
- The fourth generation rejects them.

That is the reason why in discipling our children the process is as important as the product. The right process guarantees the right product. There can be an appearance of the product being obtained without the process, but then the product cannot be passed on to another generation.

Someone once said that God has no grandchildren. A parent can be a Christian and communicate his convictions to his children. The child may believe what he is told, but until he has gone through the process of being born of the Spirit of God, he is not a Christian. The faith of Mom and Dad is insufficient for the child. The Lord must become *his* Father.

Many of us miss the kingdom of heaven by 18 inches—the distance between the heart and head. We know it intellectually but have never received Christ as our own Saviour. Until our children have gone through the process of conversion themselves, we have failed in the initial and most important step of discipling.

What is true in the conversion experience is true in the totality of the Christian life. It is the process that leads to the product. The process of each child developing his own set of reasons for believing the right things is essential in ensuring proper character.

Let me illustrate it. My son has crooked teeth and must see an orthodontist. There is nothing pleasant about getting one's teeth straightened. The metal bands are painful each time they are adjusted and an inconvenience the rest of the time. They restrict the diet and make dental hygiene difficult.

As a concerned parent I would love to spare my son the unpleasant experience of having to go to the orthodontist. But there is no way I can do that and ensure straight teeth as well. There is no way I can avoid the months and months of discomfort and produce straight teeth. The process is essential for the product.

Imparting a Value System

The Apostle Paul expresses the bases for imparting a proper value system. In his letter to the Philippians, we see necessary links in forging a spiritual chain between parents and children:

I am not saying this because I am in need, for I have learned to be content whatever the circumstances. I know what it is to be in need, and I know what it is to have plenty. I have learned the secret of being content in any and every situation, whether well fed or hungry, whether living in plenty or in want (4:11-12).

Need and plenty: The Lord blends both ingredients into every life. We will observe this in greater depth in the next chapter, but let us pause here for a moment and note two tendencies:

1. As parents, we all want to protect our children from life's hardships. As God blesses and prospers our family, we endeavor to upgrade the standard of living and shield our children from whatever struggles we perceived to be present in our childhood.

2. Every child enjoys ease and comfort more than suffering and hardship. The evolution is irresistibly upward. It is easier to adjust moving into affluence than out of it. In the student exchange program, one goes from a middle-class suburban home in the United States to a small, primitive village in the Phillipines. The Filipino comes from his village to an affluent home in the United States. Both students experience adjustments, but those of the former are far greater than those of the latter.

These two tendencies rivet our attention to the necessity of remembering Paul's example of being in need as well as having plenty. All we have is a gift from God. Paul reminded the Corinthians:

For who makes you different from anyone else? What do you have that you did not receive? And if you did receive it, why do you boast as though you did not? (1 Cor. 4:7)

The Lord also controls the circumstances that come into our lives. Like Paul, have we learned the secret of being content in any and every situation? Do we rejoice when we have little as well as when we have much? This is an important part of the Lord's value system for every believer.

How then are these values to be imparted to your children? Let me offer the following as a means of stimulating your mind toward creativity:

1. *Examine your own value system as it now is.* Earlier in the chapter, I suggested that you ask your children what they see to be your values. Have them write out, on the basis of what they observe, the things that are most important to you in life. Make sure that you emphasize that they are not to answer the question on the basis of what you say, but solely on the basis of what they perceive in you.

2. *Do not try to shelter your children from the God-ordained circumstances that become the process for proper convictions.* When our family moved to New Zealand, my daughter was crushed because none of her friends back home would continue corresponding. Her friends thought the stamps cost too much. Our hearts ached for her as she wrestled with this. Upon returning to the United States, she has maintained her relationships with her New Zealand friends in spite of the cost of stamps. Although I longed to protect her from that earlier experience of disappointment and loss of friends, she is a better person now because of it. Learning the value of relationships and the importance of maintaining them could not have been purchased more cheaply.

3. *As a family, involve yourselves in the lives of the less fortunate.* Visit the widows, orphans, and shut-ins. Serve the poor and the elderly. Good friends of mine with five of their own children constantly open their home to foster children. Sometimes they have the youngsters for a couple of weeks; sometimes for a couple of years. Not only is their family unit

richer, they are also able to permanently mark those foster children for life.

4. Help your children develop a spirit of generosity. Involve them with you in your giving program. Pray together as a family for the needs of others and then invite them to give as well. As you talk about the needs of others, and they see in you a willingness to sacrifice to meet those needs, they will adopt your pattern. This is one of the most important areas in which you can disciple your children—the values they catch from you. You impart what you are. How easy it would be if you could preach some little homily to your children and that would be it. A biblical value system is caught—not taught. Moral platitudes are simply insufficient.

5. Encourage your children to serve people. This is an important component in helping them to develop their own convictions. A number of years ago, a good friend told how he discovered this secret. He constantly encouraged his children to become involved with people. One became a candy striper at the hospital, another worked in a home for the aged. Still another assisted in a child evangelism club. The more his children learned to give of themselves, the better they understood the God of the Scriptures.

The Bible teaches that two and only two things last forever: people and the Word of God. To the degree that we give ourselves to these two eternal investments, we will be fulfilling God's purpose for our lives—and we will be reproducing the same in the lives of our progeny.

In their heart of hearts, most Christian parents want to model a biblical perspective. They want God's best for their own lives and for the lives of their children. Another side of them, however, wants to compete in the world system. Their sense of worth is tied to the opinion of people. They feel the need to be recognized by society; that their gifts and capacities are equal to the demands life places upon them. Position, prosperity, recognition; these are the world's indicators of where they stand. As their attention is focused in this direction, they drift toward an unbiblical value system.

What Jesus said is true. "No servant can serve two masters. Either he will hate the one and love the other, or he will be devoted to the one and despise the other. You cannot serve both God and Money" (Luke 16:13).

5

Spoiling Our Children

Two things stand out in the biblical narrative of Israel's redemption from the bondage of Egypt. The first is the number of miracles God performed on Israel's behalf: they began with the 10 plagues executed against Egypt to soften Pharaoh's heart; then there was the cloud by day and pillar of fire by night to lead them; the parting of the Red Sea; the destruction of the Egyptian army; water pouring out of the rock; and manna to feed them.

The second remarkable thing in the narrative is the ingratitude of the people. They constantly complained: they did not like the manna; they did not like the water; they did not like Moses. Gripe, gripe, gripe. All they did was complain.

Why? How can it be that these two phenomena exist side by side? One would think them to be mutually exclusive. It is hard to believe that such generosity could be followed by such ingratitude.

In Israel's relationship with God, the spectacular had become commonplace. They had become blind to what was taking place before their very eyes. They had seen so many miracles performed for them that they had begun to feel that God should do for them anything they desired. They forgot who they were—wretched slaves to whom God was good. And they forgot who God is—the sovereign Lord of the universe. The combination was lethal.

The Abundance of Things

Israel was like a spoiled brat. How did that happen? What was the process that brought it about? Was it the abundance of things? If that is so we are in trouble, for we have things in abundance.

Things in and of themselves, however, are not bad. It is the attitude we develop toward things that indicates whether we are in trouble or not. Paul warned Timothy, "For the love of money is a root of all kinds of evil" (1 Tim. 6:10). Note that he did not say *money* is the root of all kinds of evil; but the *love* of money. Let me develop a hypothetical case study to bring this into focus. Mr. and Mrs. Kim lived in a Third World country in which the average per capita income was $150 per year. The Kims, however, were wealthy people. Their per capita income was $500 per year. Consequently, the Kim's three children had an abundance of things—more than any of the other children in the neighborhood. They ate better, lived in a nicer home, drove a car, and were able to do things that their less fortunate neighbors were unable to do.

Later the Kims moved to the United States. Their per capita income of $500 per year makes them eligible for welfare. They have now become the poorest people in the neighborhood. They drive the same car, eat the same food, live in the same type of house, and have the same possessions. The only difference is they are now considered poor instead of rich.

It is easy to see that wealth is relative.

A Proper Perspective

A friend of mine took his daughter to Disneyland for a holiday. They spent several days viewing the sights. About half way through the experience, he noticed that his daughter was becoming indifferent to it all. As with Israel, the spectacular had become commonplace. Unlike Israel, the young girl was not old enough to understand what was happening.

If I shower upon my child his every desire, he will eventually become indifferent to my generosity. In his youth he will be unable to understand what is transpiring. Properly discipled, he will grow up able to handle extreme generosity. Improperly trained, he will have to learn his lesson the way Israel did in the wilderness.

In discipling our children, we must be careful not to spoil them. The number of things we give them will not make the difference. The perspective of life that we impart will. Here are some practical suggestions on how to impart a proper perspective:

1. Recognize God as the Author of all. James reminds his readers:

> Every good and perfect gift is from above, and coming down from the Father of the heavenly lights, who does not change like shifting shadows (1:17).

Constantly discuss as a family unit the generosity of God. Contrast it with your own unworthiness. This is what Moses tried to do with the children of Israel. Again and again you run across the word *remember* in his lectures to Israel. Remember *who* God is.

2. Recognize who you are. This is the other side of the first point. It is God's greatness contrasted by your unworthiness. Never forget who you are—a sinner to whom God has been extremely good. This need not be a morbid exercise of self-flagellation. Make it a healthy recognition of the fact that you are the product of His grace. Notice how Paul verbalizes it to the church at Ephesus:

> As for you, you were dead in your transgressions and sins, in which you used to live when you followed the ways of this world and of the ruler of the kingdom of the air, the

spirit who is now at work in those who are disobedient. All of us lived among them at one time, gratifying the cravings of our sinful nature and following its desires and thoughts. Like the rest, we were by nature objects of wrath. But because of His great love for us, God, who is rich in mercy, made us alive with Christ even when we were dead in transgressions—it is by grace you have been saved. And God raised us up with Christ and seated us with Him in the heavenly realms in Christ Jesus (Eph. 2:1-6).

3. Hold what you have with an open hand. When our children were very young, we had some missionary friends who visited us for a few days. Their child, who was the same age as one of ours, became enamored with one of our son's toys. When it was time for the family to leave, we suggested to our son that he give his toy to the visiting child. The toy had been sitting unused in the closet for months. At that moment it became my son's most prized possession. He and I had a long conversation on the subject of whose toy it was. Was it his or was it God's? If it belonged to God, what did God want him to do with it?

4. Be thankful. Jamie is a little two-year-old who lives down the street. He has become a favorite of the family. His politeness and cheerful countenance stem from an appreciation for all that is done for him. The gratitude of his mom and dad has been caught by Jamie. Rather than feeling life owes them a living, the parents are thankful for all that God and others have done for them. This thankfulness shows in Jamie's behavior.

Spiritual Atrophy
In his first epistle to the Corinthians, Paul promises:

No temptation has seized you except what is common to man. And God is faithful; He will not let you be tempted

beyond what you can bear. But when you are tempted, He
will also provide a way out so that you can stand up under it
(1 Cor. 10:13).

In this incredible verse Paul assures us of God's faithfulness. We
can be confident of three things:
1. Freedom from unique temptation.
2. Freedom from being overpowered by temptation.
3. An opportunity to escape if we so desire.

Note also that Paul says God will not allow us to be tempted
beyond what we can bear. It does not say we will not be
tempted. God does allow temptation to come into our lives—
but not more than we can handle.

Trials and tribulations are to the Christian life what hard
work is to the physical life. If you put a cast on one of your
limbs, leaving it on indefinitely, the limb will atrophy. A limb
must be used in order to be strong. This is the objective of
weight lifting and other strenuous exercise. God allows hardships
to enter our lives to build our spiritual muscles. If our
children fail to understand this, they can become embittered,
believing that God is either angry with them or has let them
down.

In the last chapter, the subject of not sheltering our children
from the God-ordained circumstances that become the process
for developing proper convictions was discussed. This is such an
important point that I mention it again here. For most of us the
absence of pain is more important than the presence of
character. For God the presence of character is more important
than the absence of pain. Trials and tribulations can be an
expression of God's love and not His neglect.

Life is impossible to understand apart from a personal
relationship with Jesus Christ. Even as Christians there is much
we cannot understand. We spoil our children when we communicate to them that life is a bowl of cherries, nothing bad
happens to Christians, or that our children should be able to
understand all that comes into their lives. Their confidence

must never be in us. It must never be in their ability to understand. It must only be in the character of God and His unfailing commitment to them.

A number of months ago my son and I were at cross purposes with one another. In my sin and pettiness, I had broken communication with him. I do not remember whose fault the problem was originally. By this time it had become my problem. Frustrated, my son went to his mother and asked her what he should do. She asked him if he thought God was big enough to get his dad's attention. He thought that God was big enough and so he prayed that the Lord would show me my error and that we would be reconciled. God answered his prayer, not because of my faithfulness, but because of God's.

I am sure that there are better ways to communicate this to our children than the trauma of this negative example. But the point remains. Children, if properly discipled, must learn to put their trust in an unfailing God.

Be Conformed

Paul is not the only one to talk about trials and tribulations. Peter writes:

> Dear friends, do not be surprised at the painful trial you are suffering, as though something strange were happening to you. But rejoice that you participate in the sufferings of Christ, so that you may be overjoyed when His glory is revealed (1 Peter 4:12-13).

To illustrate that this is not unique to the New Testament, note what God says through Isaiah. As you read it give special attention to the fact that God says "when," not "if."

> When you pass through the waters, I will be with you; and when you pass through the rivers, they will not sweep over you. When you walk through the fire, you will not be burned; the flames will not set you ablaze (Isa. 43:2).

Ours is a generation gone soft with good things. The good things are not to be blamed. The scalpel in the hand of one man destroys life; in the hand of another it saves life. The scalpel is neither good nor bad. So also with all inanimate objects. It depends on how they are used.

If we neglect to train our children in the proper use of good things, if they become spoiled and indifferent to the blessings of God, if they allow that which was intended for good to dull their senses and blur their vision, then God will have to take them through the fire. Either our children will learn to build spiritual fiber into their lives through self-discipline, or God will do it for them.

Because discipleship is caught more than taught, you will play a decisive role in these areas as you reproduce after your own kind. The attitudes you have toward God, other people, and things will be mirrored in your children. Make no mistake about it: elephants reproduce elephants, monkeys reproduce monkeys, and dogs reproduce dogs. You will reproduce after your own kind.

Paul, in his letter to the Romans, states God's objective for the believer: to be conformed to the likeness of His Son. (See Rom. 8:29.) God's plan is that people remade into the likeness of Jesus Christ inhabit "Planet Earth." As parents we are involved with Him in that process. It can be a painful experience or a delightful experience, depending on how we respond to His leadership. But His goal never changes. We will be conformed. *We* will be conformed because He wants His children conformed. As parents, you and I are God's link with our children in that process for them as well.

6

Expectations and Disappointments

My daughter, bubbling with excitement, crashed into my study with a plan. Being the sweet thing that she is, she wanted my counsel. As I sat there listening to her options, it was obvious what her course of action should be. Filled with wisdom I elected to withhold my opinion, suggesting that she was old enough to make the decision. After all, it was not a critical thing and afforded her an opportunity to learn how to make a decision and live with the consequences.

"But what do you think?" was her reply.

"No, you make the decision," I retorted.

She persisted, "If you were me, what would you do?"

"I am not you, Honey. You pray about it and do what you think is best," I answered.

Not being one easily dissuaded, she asked one more time. "If you were God, what would you do?"

"I am not God," was my equally adamant rebuttal. "You ask Him and do what you feel He wants you to do."

This terminated the conversation and she went her way. Her decision was the exact opposite of the one I would have made. As a matter of fact, the correct choice was so logical and easy to see, I became angry that she did not do it. I must confess I pouted because her decision did not coincide with mine.

Sensing that all was not well, she asked what was wrong.

"Nothing," was my reply as I seethed inside.

"Are you sure nothing is wrong?" she pressed.

Somewhat indignantly, I snapped, "Why do you push me? I told you there was nothing the matter."

"I don't know, Daddy, unless you wanted me to make a decision other than the one I made," was her insightful remark.

Her words pierced me like a sword. I grabbed her, pulled her into my arms, and confessed my folly. I had mentally developed expectations of what she should do and was disappointed when those expectations were not realized.

Expectations Are Natural

God created men to live in expectation. Paul states that he had expectations of himself as they related to his faithfulness in proclaiming the Gospel:

I eagerly expect and hope that I will in no way be ashamed, but will have sufficient courage so that now as always Christ will be exalted in my body, whether by life or by death (Phil. 1:20).

God taught Abraham to expect the fulfillment of a promised son. The fact that Abraham expected God to bring to pass that promise was the very ingredient that made him great. Note how the Apostle Paul draws our attention to this fact:

Yet he did not waver through unbelief regarding the promise of God, but was strengthened in his faith and gave glory to God, being fully persuaded that God had power to do what He had promised. This is why "it was credited to him as righteousness" (Rom. 4:20-22).

The blessed hope of Christ's return is an expectation that should grip the heart of every believer. In Paul's letter to Titus, he says, ". . . while we wait for the blessed hope—the glorious appearing of our great God and Saviour, Jesus Christ" (Titus 2:13).

Expectations deal with the future; they are something to look forward to; a desire and confidence that something will come to pass. Without expectations life becomes empty and boring and people can begin to die inside.

You can know you have expectations by virtue of the fact that you have disappointments. The disappointments indicate that you have expectations and that those expectations have been frustrated. Expectations center around two things:

1. Circumstances. My wife and I were once admonished that no family could be properly raised without camping experiences. Away from the phone and pressures of life, we were told, camping draws the family together. For us, roughing it was turning our electric blanket down to medium, but we heeded this sage counsel and planned our first camping trip.

Because we were new at it, my wife and I decided to go alone, leaving our small children with friends. Off to Big Bend National Park we traveled. As we pitched the tent, the wind came up; first gently, and then with increased velocity. One by one the surrounding tents were blown away. Frantically, we sought to salvage ours as the park ranger drove up. He suggested that the only course of action was to lie spread-eagle over the downed tent until the wind subsided. There we were, lying on the tent, praying that the wind would stop as the hours passed.

This was our baptism into camping. As the days unfolded the experience did not improve. Our expectations were not met and we vowed that camping was not our family thing.

It was not that we sat down prior to starting on the trip and articulated our expectations of the week. Though tacit, they were nonetheless there. We knew they were present by virtue of the disappointment we experienced when they were not met.

2. People. This is the second major area in which all of us have expectations. Whether it be our children, spouse, relatives, employer, employees, neighbors, or friends, we have expectations of them. Again, we may never verbalize what those expectations are, but they are there. We expect our neighbors to keep up their property. We expect our employer to be fair. We expect our children to be obedient and submissive. When they are not, we are disappointed.

This second area of expectations is the most critical. People respond negatively when expectations are not met. Conflict is the result. As parents we have expectations for our children. These are not necessarily wrong. They certainly are natural. How to handle them is extremely important as we disciple our children.

Unrealistic Expectations

An unrealistic expectation is a preconceived idea, plan, or desire centered on ourselves, on another person's response, or on how a circumstance will turn out.

Bob was a hardworking entrepreneur. He loved the market-place, and it had been good to him. The downside risks had been great, but he consistently had been able to sense where the money was to be made. His only son Jim was the apple of his eye. He dreamed of the day when Jim would come into the business with him and together they could expand the empire.

Jim, however, had his mother's temperament. He was an artist and loved the smell of paint more than the marketplace. As a lad Jim loved the idea of always being with his dad, but as he matured and became aware of his gifts, he realized that his dad's business was not for him. Bob sensed that his son wanted no part in the business and began talking about how ungrateful Jim was.

As the tension built, neither knew how to cope with it. Mom tried to mediate, but her efforts were not appreciated. Dad did not understand and classified Jim as a lazy, ungrateful son who had bitten the hand that fed him.

The problem was Bob's, not Jim's. Granted, Jim might have responded in a more gracious manner, but he lacked the perspective to understand what was unfolding. It was Dad who had created certain expectations of his son and insisted, to the point of breaking the relationship, that his expectations be met. He rationalized that his expectations of Jim were realistic and refused to recognize that it was his own, not Jim's needs that were uppermost in his mind.

The story of Bob and Jim is repeated over and over again in homes across the land. The characters and the theme may change, but the story remains the same. It is the story of parents who create hoops for their children to jump through. There may be nothing wrong with the hoops. They are no doubt the product of the parents' desire that their children have the best. But the hoops do not reflect the convictions of the children or of God who has listed His expectations in the Scriptures.

As the relationship begins to fray, the pattern is the same:

1. We suggest a course of action. If we are pious, we may even suggest that our child pray about it.

2. If our child declines, we counter by enumerating the virtues of our proposed course of action and ask that he reconsider.

3. If our child remains unconvinced, we cajole and argue with him indicating that to pass our suggestion up is to step out of God's perfect will for his life.

4. If this fails to evoke a proper response, the next step is to threaten him. Depending on how secure we feel with our child, this may vary from a veiled to an overt threat.

5. If he is so foolish that he cannot see the wisdom of our suggestion and persists in refusing to jump through our hoop, we are then left with no alternative but to punish him.

When a child is young, it is easier to impose our expectations on him. As he grows older and develops a mind of his own, it becomes increasingly harder. It is not that we do not want him to develop convictions of his own, it is just that we want those convictions to be our convictions.

For example, let's say your daughter is about to graduate from high school. It is obvious to you and your spouse where she should go to college—your alma mater. After all, you both graduated from there. That was where you met and fell in love. Nothing could be more natural.

So you ask her to pray about going there. It is not her first choice. All of her friends are going to another school—one obviously inferior. You suggest that she pray about it, but after due consideration she tells you she feels God is leading her elsewhere.

It is now time to enact step two. You take her to your alma mater for a visit, introducing her to old friends. You highlight the virtues of the campus.

She is unconvinced and as you move into step three, tension begins to develop in your relationship with her. You tell her that you feel her friends are having an unhealthy influence on her and that she ought to get away from them for awhile. You're her parents and have her best interests at heart. From your more mature vantage, you can see that your school is the best.

Still the desired response is not forthcoming. Step four involves increasing the pressure. If she insists on going with her friends, she is on her own. You will not finance a second-class education. Tears are shed and ugly things are said. You sense that the beautiful relationship you have always had with her is beginning to disintegrate. Convinced that you are right, however, you remain adamant.

If step four does not do the trick, you follow through with step five and withhold any financial assistance. She has not met your expectations and you pout. Your feelings are hurt and if you aren't careful, you end up losing your daughter.

It is impossible to eliminate expectations. Even if it were possible, it would not be desirable. Expectations are the fizz in the soda pop of life. What so frequently happens, however, is that we create *unrealistic* expectations. We look especially to those we love to meet our needs, build our egos, and affirm us in what we do. When they fail to do this to our satisfaction, we are crushed.

At the point where you first experience disappointment, ask yourself: *Whose expectations are these? Are they mine or theirs?*

*Are my expectations legitimate or have I been unfair in develop-
ing them?* Allow your disappointments to trigger a time of
evaluation and reappraisal.

The Scriptures paint a beautiful illustration of how to handle
the expectations you have of others. Word had filtered back to
Paul that the ministry he had started in Corinth was in trouble.
People were coming to the Lord's Table drunk. Christians were
hauling one another before the law courts. A man was living in
adultery with his father's wife.

Engaged in a ministry at Ephesus, Paul found it difficult to
break away and attend to the situation himself. He elected to
write a letter (1 Corinthians) and began to look for volunteers
who could represent him in Corinth. An obvious candidate was
his friend and co-laborer, Apollos. Apollos turned him down.
Note Paul's response:

> Now about our brother Apollos: I strongly urged him to
> go to you with the brothers. He was quite unwilling to go
> now, but he will go when he has the opportunity (1 Cor.
> 16:12).

Paul was not neutral about Apollos going. He "strongly
urged him" to go. He evidently felt it was feasible for Apollos
to go, or he would not have asked. Apollos said no. Shattered
expectations!

Instead of becoming hostile and embittered, Paul committed
it to God's sovereign leadership and communicated a good
attitude about it all. If the Lord wanted Apollos to go, the Lord
would communicate the same to him. I am sure Paul was
disappointed in Apollos' response, but his concept of God was
too great to allow himself to regress through the five steps I
mentioned earlier.

Realistic Expectations

What exactly are realistic expectations? To answer this question, let us observe once again that the two areas in which
people have expectations are circumstances and people.

The only realistic expectations you can have regarding circumstances are those that are *after the fact*.

I had been away from home on a trip for several weeks. As I made my way to the airport, it began to rain. I was relaxed, for I had allowed myself over an hour's margin. The harder it rained, the slower the traffic moved. When I arrived at the terminal, I rushed, suitcase in hand, out to the gate only to watch them close it in my face. Another night away from home in a motel!

If you had watched my face, you could have sensed that my expectations were thwarted and that I was disappointed. Were they realistic or unrealistic expectations? The circumstances revealed that they were unrealistic.

God is the Sovereign of the universe and He is in control of circumstances. He caused it to rain and allowed the traffic jam to prevent me from catching my plane. Why? I will probably never know. There was nothing wrong with my expecting to catch the plane. When I did not catch it, I knew it was an unrealistic expectation. You can only know whether your expectations of circumstances are realistic or not after the occurrence of the fact.

Remember also that thwarted expectations for one may be fulfilled expectations for others. I may have been disappointed because I missed my plane, but the guy on stand-by who got my seat may have been praying that his expectations would be met. When you are on a picnic and it rains, God may be answering the farmer's prayers.

What expectations regarding people are realistic? There are two kinds:

The biblical absolutes. In Scripture the Lord sets forth His expectations of how we are to live. I can expect my children to obey those absolutes. It goes without saying that God expects parents to obey them as well. All through this book, the emphasis is on example. If I do not set the pace for my children, it is impossible to expect them to do any better. "Do as I say, not as I do" always has a hollow ring to it.

Those expectations that people have of themselves. If my son tells me he will be home for dinner at 6 P.M. or that he will wash the car on Saturday, it is realistic to expect him to do it. The primary job of the discipler, whether you are discipling your child, spouse, or another person, is to help that one achieve his own expectations of what he feels God would have him do.

It must be remembered, however, that the expectations that people have of themselves must be modified by circumstances. My son may tell me that he will be home for dinner at 6 P.M. If on the way he has an accident, he and I both will have to modify our expectations.

Expectations in Perspective

A couple more thoughts may help give a proper perspective to our expectations as we seek to influence our children toward godly living:

1. Expectations must be centered in the Lord. David captured this thought when he said: "My soul, wait thou only upon God; for my expectation is from Him" (Ps. 62:5, KJV).

Ultimately, only God can meet our expectations. People will disappoint us. Instead of seeking the fulfillment of our needs in another person, the Lord wants us to seek them in Him. He has created us. He knows what the deepest inner needs of our lives are and only He is equipped to meet them.

People can never meet the primary needs in our lives. They can only meet secondary needs. If we can grab hold of this thought and apply it to our lives, it will set us free. Instead of looking to our children to meet our needs and then becoming hurt and disappointed when they do not, we can relax in the Lord and concentrate on seeing that their needs are met.

2. Expectations are a two-way street. Just as we have expectations of our children—both realistic and unrealistic—so they have the same of us. How we respond to the thwarted expectations we have of them plays a significant role in their training.

For instance, make sure that you keep your word to your children. Remember, your promise to them is the expectation you have of yourself. This is a realistic expectation that they have of you and they are going to want to hold you to it.

Your son asks you to take him to a ball game. The date is several weeks away and you eagerly commit yourself. As you move closer to the game, your schedule tightens and you begin to suggest alternatives to your son. God-ordained circumstances don't cause the trouble. Rather the trouble is with your priorities, and your son can tell the difference. Make sure that the expectations you have for your children are the same kind you have for yourself.

7

Positive and Negative Commands

It was on Mt. Sinai that God gave Moses the Ten Commandments. As you read through them, you notice that there are eight negative and two positive commands. Commandment number four is the first of the two positives: "Remember the Sabbath Day by keeping it holy" (Ex. 20:8). Commandment number five is the second of the two positives: "Honor your father and your mother, so that you may live long in the land the Lord your God is giving you" (v. 12).

As you reflect on the difference between the positive and negative commands, it is immediately apparent that you can easily evaluate yourself regarding the negative ones. For example, if I say, "Thou shalt not take the name of the Lord thy God in vain" (Ex. 20:7, KJV), you know immediately whether you have ever done it. If I quote commandment eight, "You shall not steal," you know whether you have stolen or not.

The positive commandments, however, are not so easy. Let us try commandment number five on for size. "Honor your father and your mother." If you were asked to evaluate your performance, how would you answer? Most would probably say, "Yes, no, well sometimes, maybe not as I ought, I think so, compared to what?"

Compared to what? That is precisely the problem with the

positive commandments. They are difficult to evaluate in your life and impossible to evaluate in the lives of others.

A classic example is the fourth commandment, "Remember the Sabbath Day by keeping it holy." In your mind's eye you can see the Jewish leadership sitting around the table trying to come to grips with it. How do they keep the day holy?

One responds, "You can't show up on the job, for it says not to work."

"Good, let's make a list and put that down," says another.

Another says, "What about my wife? She lives on the job." A good question.

Still another answers, "It means no meal preparation that day." That nails it down; record it!

"I have some chickens," says another. "What do I do with eggs laid on the Sabbath?"

"Wow! How do we handle that?"

After a long discussion they concluded that if the eggs were laid for commercial purposes, that constituted work and the eggs must be destroyed. If, however, they were laid for reproductive purposes, that was not work and the eggs could be eaten.

By the time they were done, these Jewish leaders had long lists of what could and could not be done on the Sabbath. You cannot fault their motive. It was a sincere attempt to evaluate a positive command. The problem was, by the time of our Lord Jesus, these extra-biblical rules became coequal in authority with the commandments of God. Jesus kept all of God's laws, but felt no obligation to keep these extra-biblical rules. As the Gospel narrative unfolds, you notice that Jesus' unwillingness to conform to their ideas on how the Sabbath should be kept was an important factor in their decision that He must die.

This is illustrative of what can so easily happen with the positive commandments. You simply cannot evaluate them in the lives of others. When you do so you become pharisaical.

It is true that keeping the negative commands is an indication of whether I am keeping the positive commands. For example,

Jesus said, "If you love Me, you will obey what I command" (John 14:15). If I love God, I will not break any of the negative commandments such as killing, stealing, and committing adultery. But remember, that is a one-way street. Not breaking the negative commands does not mean I am loving God.

A good example of this is the command not to divorce my wife. If I love my wife, I will not divorce her, but not divorcing my wife does not mean that I love her. So also in our relationship with God. If I love Him I will obey Him, but obedience is not motivated only by love. There are a number of other reasons why I may obey God, such as fear, the promise of reward, and the desire to impress others.

Purpose of the Positive Commands

Because the negative commands are crisp and easy to evaluate, good civil law is stated negatively. In the 1960s the United States began to make exceptions to this with affirmative action programs, but invariably they ended in litigation. Positively stated commands are impossible to evaluate and therefore impossible to legislate.

If this is so, then why does God introduce positive commandments? Negative commandments deal with outward performance; positive commandments with inner attitude. Nowhere is this more clearly seen than in Isaiah 1:11-20:

> "The multitude of your sacrifices—what are they to Me?" says the Lord. "I have more than enough of burnt offerings, of rams and the fat of fattened animals; I have no pleasure in the blood of bulls and lambs and goats. When you come to meet with Me, who has asked this of you, this trampling of My courts? Stop bringing meaningless offerings! Your incense is detestable to Me. New Moons, Sabbaths and convocations—I cannot bear your evil assemblies. Your New Moon festivals and your appointed feasts My soul hates. They have become a burden to Me; I am weary of bearing them. When you spread out your hands in prayer, I will hide My eyes from you; even if you offer many

prayers, I will not listen. Your hands are full of blood; wash and make yourselves clean. Take your evil deeds out of My sight! Stop doing wrong, learn to do right! Seek justice, encourage the oppressed. Defend the cause of the fatherless, plead the case of the widow.

"Come now, let us reason together," says the Lord. "Though your sins are like scarlet, they shall be as white as snow; though they are red as crimson, they shall be like wool. If you are willing and obedient, you will eat the best from the land; but if you resist and rebel, you will be devoured by the sword." For the mouth of the Lord has spoken.

Israel met the requirement of the ceremonial law as far as outward performance was concerned. The Israelites became a burden instead of a blessing to the Lord because their hearts were not into the real meaning of the sacrifices. The Lord is interested in the heart, not just the performance.

This is not to suggest that God is not interested in performance; quite the contrary. In this same Isaiah passage, He tells Israel to cease with the sacrifices, but nowhere in Scripture does He suggest that they should cease being moral—wrong motives notwithstanding.

The negative commandments, however, do not give an accurate reading on the heart, and the heart is extremely important to God. The Lord knows exactly what is going on in our hearts and can read every thought and intent. The writer to the Hebrews illustrates this point:

Nothing in all creation is hidden from God's sight. Everything is uncovered and laid bare before the eyes of Him to whom we must give account (4:13).

In this respect the Lord is different than we are. Unlike Him we cannot judge the motives of others. We even have difficulty judging our own motives. Paul bears witness to this when he reminds the Corinthians,

I care very little if I am judged by you or by any human court; indeed, I do not even judge myself. My conscience is clear, but that does not make me innocent. It is the Lord who judges me (1 Cor. 4:3-4).

Only the Lord can accurately evaluate and judge our response to the positive commandments. We must search our own hearts regarding them, but never fall into the trap of the Pharisees and seek to obey the commandments merely for others to see our good works.

Purpose of the Negative Commands

If the positive commandments are so important to God, if they only give an accurate reading of the heart, then why does God give the negative commandments at all? There are two major reasons for their presence in the Scriptures.

First they express God's moral character in such a way that all mankind can know the performance He expects. Negative commands are easy to evaluate and all people can readily see how they are to conduct their affairs. They also act as a schoolmaster to teach us our need for Christ. Paul, in writing to the Galatians says, "So the Law was put in charge to lead us to Christ that we might be justified by faith" (Gal. 3:24).

Second they serve as signposts or indicators in the Christian life as to what the positive commandments ought to look like when lived out. For example:

- If I love my wife—I will not divorce her.
- If I love my children—I will not provoke them to wrath.
- If I love my neighbor—I will not kill, steal, or lie to him.
- If I love my God— I will not take His name in vain.

Thus the negative commandments guide me in my quest to love God with all my heart, soul, and mind.

What is Wrong with Being a Pharisee?

There was probably no group of people that Jesus was harder

on than the Pharisees. Again and again He showed them that they were mishandling the Word of God. One such meeting Jesus had with them is recorded in Mark 7:1-13. It is worth our investigation:

The Pharisees and some of the teachers of the Law who had come from Jerusalem gathered around Jesus and ²saw some of His disciples eating food with "unclean"—that is, ceremonially unwashed—hands. ³(The Pharisees and all the Jews do not eat unless they give their hands a ceremonial washing, holding to the tradition of the elders. ⁴When they come from the market-place they do not eat unless they wash. And they observe many other traditions, such as the washing of cups, pitchers, and kettles.)

⁵So the Pharisees and teachers of the Law asked Jesus, "Why don't Your disciples live according to the tradition of the elders instead of eating their food with 'unclean' hands?"

⁶He replied, "Isaiah was right when he prophesied about you hypocrites; as it is written: 'These people honor Me with their lips, but their hearts are far from Me. ⁷They worship Me in vain; their teachings are but rules taught by men.' ⁸You have let go of the commands of God and are holding on to the traditions of men."

⁹And He said to them: "You have a fine way of setting aside the commands of God in order to observe your own traditions! ¹⁰For Moses said, 'Honor your father and mother,' and 'Anyone who curses his father or mother must be put to death.' ¹¹But you say that if a man says to his father or mother: 'Whatever help you might otherwise have received from me is Corban' (that is, a gift devoted to God), ¹²then you no longer let him do anything for his father or mother. ¹³Thus you nullify the Word of God by your tradition that you have handed down. And you do many things like that."

As you read about this encounter in Mark 7, you immediately sense the conflict. The issue is the traditions of man versus the commandments of God. Read back through the narrative one more time and note in verses 3, 5, 7, 8, 9, and 13 the references to the commandments, or Word of God.

Jesus carefully kept the commandments of God, but felt under no obligation to keep the commandments of men. This is not to say that He broke the law of the state. At His trial the civil court could find no fault with Him. We too, in passages such as Romans 13 and 1 Peter 2, are admonished to obey the law of the land.

The problem with the Pharisees, however, was different. They had taken the positive commandments (such as keeping the Sabbath), interpreted what obeying them ought to include, and insisted that people, in order to be godly, keep not only what God commanded, but what they added to the commandments as well. Jesus also pointed out to the Pharisees how they conveniently ignored God's commands with their rationalization and encouraged the people to break His commandments in order to obtain their own purposes.

This twofold problem of adding to God's Word, as well as breaking His express commandments, gives us a strategic clue as to what to avoid in discipling children. For example:

1. The Pharisees required people to do unnecessary things. Jesus told the Pharisees (Mark 7:7) that Isaiah was right when he prophesied about "you" hypocrites: "Their teachings are but rules taught by men." The following illustration might clarify the problem and make it applicable to your situation:

You develop a conviction that you should attend a certain number of church meetings each week. So far so good. But no place in the Bible does it say how many meetings each week you must attend; neither does it say you cannot develop your own conviction on the number. So for you it is five: three on Sunday and two during the week.

When your children are young, they naturally follow your conviction. When you attend they attend. As they move into their teens (maybe earlier), they begin to have ideas of their own. They say they would like to attend only two meetings a week. It is right here that there is potential for conflict. Are children less spiritual because they want to go to two rather than five meetings? Remember, godliness is an inner quality of the heart. It cannot be accurately measured by the meetings attended. Conversely, if forced to attend the meetings against their will, you run a good chance of destroying whatever commitment the children may have.

The Bible is the Christian's only rule of faith and practice. This means that the Bible, not man, determines what the spiritual life looks like. Because the Bible does not speak to all of our opinions as to what is right and wrong, and because we cannot evaluate in another the heart attitude expressed in the positive commands, we yield to the temptation to become Pharisees. We make our own rules and teach them as the doctrines of God. As a result we run the risk of either driving our children away from the faith we so desperately want them to embrace, or we reproduce after our own kind and they too become Pharisees.

Moral wrong can be determined through inference in the Bible, but you must be careful with your logic. For example, there is no commandment in Scripture prohibiting abortion. This does not mean, however, that the believer is free to practice abortion. The inference of the Scriptures clearly prohibits it. We reason thus:

- "You shall not murder" (Ex. 20:13).
- A baby is alive at conception.
- Abortion is murder.

The following is an example of misusing inference and thus determining wrong:

- "Avoid every kind of evil" (1 Thes. 5:22).
- Movies appear to be evil.
- Abstain from movies.

The statement "movies appear to be evil" is not a statement of fact like "a baby is alive at conception." Rather it is a value judgment. You may get all Christians to agree with you that *"some* movies appear to be evil," but in all probability, they will not all agree on which movies belong in the "some" category.

Parents face this problem in raising children. If it is not movies or the number of times they should attend church, then it is something else. In discipling your children, you will want to reason with them on these issues. Pray together regarding God's will. To the degree that you make the decision for them, however, you stifle the discipling process. The goal is for them to desire what is right and to make the right decision themselves.

If in all of this you feel somewhat frightened, you are beginning to understand the problem. Walking by faith is difficult. It is never any harder than in the area of trusting God for the discipling of your children. The Scripture teaches us that we should have a profound distrust of ourselves apart from God's help and direction. For example, Paul says: "Indeed, in our hearts we felt the sentence of death. But this happened that we might not rely on ourselves but on God, who raises the dead" (2 Cor. 1:9). It matters not how profound your distrust of yourself may be, your distrust of others may be even greater.

Your temptation is to build fences around your children with the extra-biblical rules. You have learned through personal experiences that God can get your attention, but you aren't so sure about your children.

It is impossible to disciple your children without first trusting God to do the building in their lives. "Unless the Lord builds the house, its builders labor in vain" (Ps. 127:1a). Are you willing to pray that God will bring experiences into your children's lives that will provide them their own opportunities to apply the Scriptures?

2. The Pharisees broke the commandments of God. Jesus accused them of rejecting the commandments of God (see Mark 7:9). Here is a hypothetical situation for an up-to-date illustration:

You're in a hurry to get to your destination and you exceed

the speed limit appreciably. The Apostle Paul clearly teaches that you are to obey the law of the land (see Rom. 13), and your would-be disciple sitting next to you in the front seat asks you about it. You glibly answer, "We are not under the law but under grace."

You are reading a current news magazine. One article tells of the fraud and waste in government. Another article draws attention to the increasing number of people who are cheating on their income tax by not reporting all their earned income. The Holy Spirit convicts you of the fact that you do not record all of your income, but you justify yourself with the argument that the government gives to people who refuse to work and misappropriates and squanders what is left.

The Pharisees had a double-edged problem. They taught as doctrine the commandments of men and they rejected the commandments of God. One does not have to be a genius to see that a Pharisee cannot produce a disciple of Jesus Christ.

8

Disciplining Our Children

The sun streamed through the windows as the mother sat in the living room with her son. Hanging from the ceiling, drinking in the sun's rays, was a large spider plant—its tentacles reaching down to the floor. The little boy took one of the clusters in his hand and looked at it.

"Don't pull the leaves off," cautioned his mother.

Looking her right in the eye, the lad snapped off two of the leaves.

"Son, stop that," said his mother.

Off went two more leaves.

"If you do that one more time, Mommie will have to spank you," warned his mother.

This time the plant lost three leaves.

Angered by such flagrant disobedience, the mother harshly intoned, "I told you to stop that!"

Still another handful was jerked off.

"Stop that," screamed his mother.

Again the plant suffered loss at the hand of the child.

Now livid with anger, the mother reached over and swatted the boy so hard it knocked him down. Crying, he rushed out of the room.

The child's problem was: he did not know when his mother meant what she said and when she did not. Next time, would he be spanked on the third warning, or would it be the eighth? That would depend on Mom's frustration level at that given moment, and there was no way that even she could predict when it would be reached.

A child's concept of God is appreciably shaped by his parents. If Mom and Dad are unpredictable—if they are vindictive and inconsistent—it will carry over into the child's image of God. How we handle our child ought to be an accurate reflection of how God handles us.

This is especially true when it comes to disciplining. *Discipline* is the root word from which we get *disciple.* As parents we never grow out of the need to be disciplined. However, the authority figure for parents is now primarily God. When our children are disciplined, the authority figure is primarily the parents. How we discipline our children is extremely important in our discipling of them.

In the opening story, the mother was not fair with her child. She may have been frustrated, but he was also. There was no way he could predict her behavior. With God we always know where we stand. For example, Paul says:

> Do not be deceived: God cannot be mocked. A man reaps what he sows. The one who sows to please his sinful nature, from that nature will reap destruction; the one who sows to please the Spirit, from the Spirit will reap eternal life (Gal. 6:7-8).

From the smallest transgression to the greatest of sins, we can always count on reaping what we sow. The reliability of God in dealing with sin assures our hearts that He is also reliable in dealing with salvation. Conversely, if parents' negative promises cannot be trusted, what assurance does the child have that the positive ones can? As the parent properly disciplines, the child's confidence and assurance is strengthened.

Correction versus Punishment

God's chastisement of His people is never punitive; it is always corrective. The punishment for our sins was nailed to the Cross. That was the purpose of Jesus' dying. Solomon understood this when he wrote:

> My son, do not despise the Lord's discipline and do not resent His rebuke, because the Lord disciplines those He loves, as a father the son he delights in (Prov. 3:11-12).

The Lord sets the standard for Christian parents. Jesus, who died for our sins, also died for the sins of our children. When He rebukes us it is for corrective purposes. As Christ's representatives to our children, we should rebuke them for corrective purposes also.

Never punish your children. This doesn't mean you should never spank them. Again Solomon writes, "He who spares the rod hates his son, but he who loves him is careful to discipline him" (Prov. 13:24). It does mean that your discipline is to be motivated by an effort to help them do right rather than to punish them for doing wrong.

We should never correct our children in anger. All of God's anger for our sins was expressed against Christ at Golgotha. As long as we are angry with our children, it is our problem, not theirs. Motive is decisive. We do not punish to get even with them for wronging us. We *correct* them so they will again walk the proper path.

- Punishment is reactionary—correction is creative.
- Punishment is done with you in mind—correction is done with them in mind.
- When you punish you represent yourself—when you correct you represent the Lord.
- When you punish you blur discipline—when you correct you sharpen discipline.

Correction always has focus to it. This is what discipline is all about. We discipline our children as part of a larger process in teaching them how to discipline themselves. To the degree that people are able to discipline themselves, they have no need to be disciplined by others. Hopefully, as we train our children in godliness, parental discipline will become increasingly unnecessary. The older our children get, the more they should be able to handle their own discipline.

A word about mercy is in order here. If the objective of discipline were punishment, then mercy would be an important consideration—for God is merciful. His mercy toward us is not displayed by His reneging on what He promised. Rather His mercy is seen in taking our due punishment and laying it on Christ.

Correction, on the other hand, doesn't need to consider mercy. For the objective of correction is not punishment for wrongdoing, but assistance in doing what is right. Assistance does not require mercy simply because assistance is motivated by the other person's best interest. Whenever you hear talk of mercy, you know you have strayed from biblical discipline.

Let us return to the illustration of the mother who spanked her son for pulling leaves from the spider plant. Ideally, a spanking is administered to help the child obey his mother and to learn not to ruin the plant. The spanking is not to punish the child for wrongdoing. Rather it is designed with his best interest in mind. If there is a better way to teach the boy this dual lesson, then that way should be used. You can see, then, that mercy is not a consideration. The boy's well-being, not the mode of correction, is the objective.

Creativity is essential in correcting our children. What works for an 18-month-old child may not work for an 18-year-old child. What works for one 4-year-old child may not work for another 4-year-old-child. In all cases, however, the objective is the same: eventual self-discipline.

One day Ron brought home a large fan to help cool the house. The first thing he did was gather his three young daughters into the kitchen, turn on the fan, and insert a raw carrot. Pieces of carrot flew all over the kitchen. He then turned to his daughters and said, "Sweethearts, don't put your fingers in the fan. You can see what will happen if you do." Their saucer-sized eyes assured him that he had made his point.

Bill had a son who lied to him. Each time the boy lied, Bill spanked him. One day as they were chatting, Bill asked him why he lied so much. "Because I am afraid of your spankings," was the boy's reply. He had such a fear of his dad's spankings that he would lie every time his dad investigated any infraction. Bill asked him, "Would you stop lying if I promised never to spank you again?" The boy said yes, and Bill said that that ended the problem.

As Bill and I talked about it, he observed that there were ways other than spankings to discipline his son. If the boy was so fearful of spankings that he would lie, Bill would simply choose an alternate mode of correction.

In all of these cases, correction, not punishment, was the motive. The objective was teaching the child how to discipline himself. This is the goal of the Christian parent as he seeks to disciple his child.

Principles of Discipline

What are some principles to keep in mind when correcting your child? If discipleship is the goal of discipline, what are some constants we as parents can incorporate? Here are a few:

1. *Do not be whimsical or capricious.* There are two major areas to guard against in this. One is in the rules you make. There are many things that are either unsafe or wrong that you have to deny your child. It is hard to remain positive. Whenever your child asks for something, try to make your initial response yes. Only say no if you have to.

The other area has to do with consistency. The lady in the opening story of this chapter is an example of being inconsistent. The ability to be consistent is both important and difficult, especially if you have a persistent child. Say what you mean and mean what you say.

2. Keep the rules to a minimum. Many parents have three easy to understand rules for their children, namely, three rules that if broken will cause them to be disciplined: They are not to lie, disobey, or be disrespectful. The more rules you have, the harder it is for both you and your children to keep track of them. As much as possible, you want your relationship with your children to be based on the positive. Rules generally deal with what cannot be done.

3. Allow your child the freedom to be honest. I remember when growing up that this was one thing I appreciated so much in my father. Whenever I felt he was wrong or unfair, I had the freedom to come to him. As long as I was respectful, he heard me out.

The writer of Proverbs says, "He who answers before listening—that is his folly and his shame" (18:13). It is better to hear your child out before the discipline rather than after. To do so will save a lot of grief.

4. Be willing to admit you are wrong. All of us make mistakes. When you make one, admit it. You cannot fool your child; he knows when you are wrong. You may find it hard on your pride, but go to him and say, "Son, I am sorry; will you forgive me?" You will not lose your child's respect in doing this—you will gain it. Your willingness to admit when you are wrong will gain you credibility in the discipling process.

5. Seek to solve the basic problem. This is the flip side of saying do not nitpick. I believe Paul had this in mind when he said, "Fathers, do not exasperate your children" (Eph. 6:4).

Let us say for example that your child is habitually late for meals. Instead of rebuking him each time it happens, ask the Lord to reveal the basic problem. You notice that a pattern develops. He butts into people's conversations. He walks away from people as they are talking to him. The root problem is his insensitivity to people. Being late for meals is a symptom.

Rather than attacking symptoms, ask God to give you the wisdom to help him with the root cause.

6. Allow your child to help evaluate his disobedience. Talk the whole problem through with him. Let him cross-examine himself and come up with the solution. Remember, your goal is to help him discipline himself. If he is teachable, the more he is involved in the process, the better the chance for results.

7. Never accuse your child; always ask. This is hard to practice when you feel you have the goods on him. Speaking of the Messiah, Isaiah said, "He will not judge by what He sees with His eyes, or decide by what He hears with His ears" (Isa. 11:3b). Often the eyes and the ears deceive. If Jesus refused to judge by using them, we should follow His example.

This is why it is best to ask. If the child lies, pray that the Lord will help him face up to his lie. It is better to have your child know that you trust him, even when that trust may be misplaced, than to falsely accuse him and thus communicate a lack of trust. You should teach him that ultimately he must answer to God who knows and understands the heart.

8. Make sure you and your spouse present a unified front. The child may play one parent against another, but to the degree he succeeds, he becomes insecure. Together with your spouse, you both are his authority figures. When you are at cross-purposes with one another, the child feels uncertain.

If you sense that you and your partner are not together, suspend judgment until you can get alone and talk about it. As Jesus said, "Every city or household divided against itself will not stand" (Matt. 12:25).

9. Pray that when your child does wrong, he will get caught. Not only do my wife and I pray this for our children, we pray this prayer in front of our children. "Every other child may cheat on the exam or steal from the store and get away with it, but Lord, not my child." We pray that our children will learn to hate sin. One of the best ways for them to learn this is to get caught when they do wrong. One of the most horrible things that can happen to children is for them to get away with wrong and thus deceive themselves into believing that there is no accounting for sin.

10. *Never ridicule or belittle your child.* For most people, their sense of self-worth is fragile. As we disciple our children, we need to build, not destroy that sense. When we belittle, we communicate rejection, not correction. Correction is for the purpose of restoration. Ridicule defeats this purpose.

Love Cancels Many Sins

If handled properly, discipline can play a positive role in discipling. When misused, it can destroy all other efforts in that direction. For this reason it is essential that you be creative as you correct. Pray that the Holy Spirit will deliver you from the trap of being negative, punitive, or reactionary.

All of us make mistakes with our children. It would be impossible to record the number of times I have had to go to my children and apologize. Fortunately, they somehow realize that I, like they, am fallible. I take great solace and encouragement in Peter's promise that "love covers over a multitude of sins" (1 Peter 4:8b).

9

Family Devotions

"Hey, Dad, can we read out of that neat book again tonight?"

The words startled the father, as they interrupted the flow of family conversation around the evening meal. It was obvious that Johnnie's mind was elsewhere.

"Sure, Son," replied the father with a smile. "Why don't you go get it?"

It was this kind of response on the part of Johnnie that confirmed to his mom and dad that God answered prayers. They had observed on many occasions the ruts families get into with family devotions. Just recently they were in the home of friends and noticed the perfunctory way they read the Bible and prayed at the table. Even more sad was the bored look on the faces of the children. It was obvious they could hardly wait to finish and break away from it. How easy it is to fall into that kind of rut. "Lord, help us to help our children so that our times with You will be fresh and exciting."

Johnnie ran to get the large volume from the coffee table and lugged it in to the waiting family.

"Let's see, kids, where did we leave off last time?"

"I remember, Daddy," squealed the little girl. "It was where that bird was attacking those animals."

She was referring to Bill Gothard's *Character Sketches*. Dad would embellish them with his own anecdotes and then together they would discuss the lessons which were in the stories.

Probably most important to Mom and Dad was the fact that devotions had become the children's idea. They could hardly wait each evening for another episode.

Variety

A number of factors must be considered when developing family devotions if they are going to remain fresh and interesting. Remember, we are spending time with the King of kings—the sovereign Lord of the universe. To be flippant or indifferent would be sacrilege and to communicate this to our children, is to sin against them in the worst way. It would be perpetuating the lie of family devotions being relatively unimportant.

Prayerfully think through how you are going to lead the family in devotions. Include these facts in your considerations:

1. The age of your children. When the children are young, their attention span is short. Devotions should be short and lots of stories should be used. As your children grow older, the length of time can be increased and you can move more into conceptual material. Books like *Mere Christianity* (Macmillan) by C.S. Lewis and *My Utmost for His Highest* (Dodd) by Oswald Chambers are examples of conceptual books. Be sure and grade your time and material to the level of the children.

If there is a wide age span among the children, then gear the family time mostly to the youngest and involve the older ones in the preparation. Then you can plan to meet individually with the older children for morning or evening devotions.

2. The spiritual maturity of your children. If you and your family are new to the Christian faith, use material that will build a good foundation for your belief. A simple question-and-answer Bible study like *Lessons in Christian Living* (NavPress) done together around the table as a family will introduce you to the basic tenets of the Christian faith.

You need to grow in understanding and knowledge of the doctrines in the Bible. It is interesting to note that this is the admonition of Paul in most of his epistles. He was not writing to churches full of people who were saturated with knowledge, but rather to young, recent converts from heathenism. For them application was not so much a problem as it was learning the ABCs of the faith.

If, for example, you have never completely read through the Bible, you may want to do that. Use a fresh, free-flowing translation. J.B. Phillips' *New Testament in Modern English* and the *Living Bible* are good for this. When the time comes to study a passage, then you will want to use something a little more scholarly, such as the *New International Version,* the *Authorized Version* or the *New American Standard Bible.*

3. The saturation of your children. My children are a perfect example here. They were raised in a family that took the faith seriously. During their formative years, we had young men and women live with us for training in the Christian life. All of them were committed Christians.

Our home is a center of ministry. We talk about the Bible all the time. The children go to a Christian school where all their academic subjects are related to the Scriptures. They attend church, Sunday school, and so on. We have to be careful lest they are fed such a rich diet that they regurgitate, and the latter end is worse than the former condition. Knowledge and understanding are not their needs. They need experience and application. As parents, this is the challenge facing us.

4. The use of good material. There is a wealth of good material fresh on the market that you will want to look over. The following are some books that we have enjoyed as a family.

For the very young, Moody Press publishes *The Bible in Pictures for Little Children* by Kenneth N. Taylor. Records that the children can play themselves accompany the book.

A favorite of our children between the ages 3-10 was the *Arch Book Series* published by Concordia. The stories of the Bible are put in simple but interesting poetry. There are a large number of them available, all tastefully done.

The Children's Bible (Golden Press) and Catherine Vos' *The Child's Story Book* (Eerdmans) are also good for children in the preteen years. For variety in this age span, you may want to look at *Little Visits with God* and *More Little Visits with God* published by Concordia. They emphasize a moral truth by telling a story and relating it to a verse of Scripture.

There is a fabulous *Jungle Doctor* series (Moody Press) by Paul White. Dr. White was a missionary who taught biblical truths using animal characters. There are about 17 books in the series.

From an entirely different approach, Bill Gothard uses animals to communicate spiritual truths. In *Character Sketches* Volume I and II, he first makes a point using the habits of an animal or bird, and then illustrates the point with a Bible character.

Do not feel that you must complete a whole book before changing to something fresh. The materials are a means to an end—not an end in themselves. Use them, but do not become bound by them.

The Place of Prayer

We discussed the importance of prayer in motivating our children toward righteousness in chapter 1. We repeat and expand on this to make a point. Prayer is the work of God. It is the single most important thing you can do in discipling your children. Begin in prayer, continue in prayer, and end in prayer.

We can pray for our grandchildren many years before they are born. My teenage daughter and I pray regularly for the man she will someday marry (whom she probably has not yet met) and for her children. We pray together that the Lord will choose her husband, that the young man will have a heart for God, that they will be kept in purity, and that together they will glorify God.

Prayer for children should continue after their marriage and before their children arrive. Pray for the fruit of their union—

that the Lord will be gracious and protect your grandchildren physically, spiritually, mentally, and emotionally. Pray that God will do for them what He did for Jeremiah. "Before I formed you in the womb I knew you, before you were born I set you apart; I appointed you as a prophet to the nations" (Jer. 1:5).

Pray for the child daily during the pregnancy. After his birth pray daily for the child lying there in the crib. Pray for his future—that he will grow up to know God and enjoy Him forever.

At every stage of the child's development, bathe him in prayer. Remember the words from Scripture:

> For our struggle is not against flesh and blood, but against the rulers, against the authorities, against the powers of this dark world and against the spiritual forces of evil in the heavenly realms (Eph. 6:12).

It is a spiritual battle we are in. Our children need defense against not just flesh and blood, but spiritual forces in high places. The forces of hell seek to destroy the work God is doing in our children. Prayer is an indispensable weapon in this conflict.

1. Pray for your children in your private devotions. Pray for them during your extended times of fellowship with God. Pray daily with your spouse for all your children and bring their needs before your heavenly Father. Pray for them as you drive to work, as you clean house, and as you spend time in recreation. "Pray continually" (1 Thes. 5:17).

2. Pray during personal time with your family. As you tuck your children in at night, lie down next to them for a few moments and talk over the day—what happened at school, with friends, at play. Then make sure your prayer time is natural and spontaneous. Avoid making it seem like a ritual.

As children grow older, try having morning devotions with

each one individually. The two of you will want to retreat to a solitary place and spend time in prayer and the Word of God. A time problem will threaten this aspect of your discipling, so don't make it a long, drawn-out event. Your goal is not only time together before the Lord, but the establishment of a habit in his life.

3. Be available to the family when they want time. As the children move into their teen years, they will want to choose the time to be with you. It may be to discuss a crisis such as a disagreement with friends. They may have a special concern and need your counsel. Sometimes they may simply want to talk. Relish these moments. Lay aside whatever you are doing (within reason) and lock into their need. Some of your best times in prayer with your children will come as a result of your being available to them.

4. Look for answers to prayer. Expectation should follow supplication. As you are fellowshiping with the family, ask them to share answers to prayer. A friend of mine was having some financial problems. He gathered his family around him, shared the need, and together they prayed. As each need was met, he called it to the family's attention and together they thanked the Lord for answered prayer.

As your family prays for specific things, and God later answers and meets those needs, remember to talk about them and God's faithfulness. It is important not only to pray, but to look for God's answers to prayer.

Surrender

Submission to the Lord's perfect plan for our lives is central to worship. Family devotions are often called the *family altar.* It is a good term, for there you take all that is sacred to you and lay it on the altar before God.

Abraham had such an experience when the Lord asked him to take his son Isaac and offer him as a sacrifice. I am sure this was not easy for Abraham. He no doubt did a lot of soul-searching as he made his way up Mt. Moriah. But his act of surrender opened the way for God's blessing.

In a thousand little ways, God calls upon us to take our Isaacs (our plans, dreams, aspirations) to Mt. Moriah—to the family altar. You may not feel comfortable sharing every struggle and trial with your children. The Scriptures don't call upon you to do that. They must, however, see you in an attitude of surrender. This is the heart of devotion to Jesus. Your children will observe and learn from you.

If there has never been a time in your life when you have done this, now is the time to begin. It is between you and God. It cannot be done in concert with your mate.

One by one give back to the Lord all of the things that are precious to you. Begin with your spouse. "Lord, You know how much my beloved means to me and the hole that would be left in my life if she were taken. But I acknowledge that she is a gift from You, and You can have her anytime You in Your wisdom want to take her."

From there go to your children. Offer them back to the Lord, one at a time. Then surrender your health, your sight, the ability to reason, the absence of pain, etc. Next return to Him all of your possessions, dreams, goals, hopes. Think about their importance to you, and then bring them to Mt. Moriah.

The family altar is more than an activity. It has as its foundation lives yielded to God. When you and your family gather together in the presence of God, your worship is simply a verbalization of your lifestyle.

10

Ministering Together as a Family

Howard's teenage daughter looked regal as she moved from guest to guest offering them a refill of their beverages. You could sense the excitement and anticipation that filled her whole being. She was actually ministering with her mother and dad in presenting the Gospel to some uncommitted friends.

She had worked hard for several weeks in preparation for this banquet. First there were the invitations. Each one had to be hand-addressed. Then there were the decorations, the meal preparation, and the cleaning and arranging of their home. They were not chores that *had* to be done. Her heart was in them; so were her prayers. A great deal of family time had been spent praying for each guest prior to his arrival.

At long last the night had arrived. As she made her last round picking up the used dishes, she heard her dad introduce the speaker. Retreating to just inside the kitchen, she sat down to pray and listen to the speaker. He was a man from the marketplace who had met the Master and had a story to tell. "Lord, touch the hearts of these wonderful people," she prayed as the speaker brought his story to a close.

Then it was all over. The guests were gone. She was alone with her family as they talked over what had transpired. An opportunity had been given to respond to the claims of Christ.

Those guests who felt so inclined placed their name tags in the hand of the speaker as they left the house. One by one the family prayed over this small collection of name tags that had been left. "Lord, reveal Yourself to Mr. Jones; help him to understand what You are doing in his heart . . . 'being confident of this, that He who began a good work in you will carry it on to completion until the day of Christ Jesus'" (Phil. 1:6).

It was a special evening for this family unit, but one that was not unique. They had ministered together before and they would be doing it again. Their daughter was an integral part of the ministry. It would not be necessary to convince her of the need to share her faith with others. She was learning to do it as she ministered with Mom and Dad.

People Are Important

"Come on, gang," hollered Billy, as he and his companions raced through the door heading straight for the cookie jar. After making short work of its contents, they roared down the hall to Billy's room talking about who would be first with the small race-car game. As they broke through the bedroom door, his mother finally caught up with them. She was livid as she vented her anger over the trail of cookie crumbs and noisy children who had disrupted an otherwise tranquil house. Deflated, they made their way out of the house as Jimmy said, "Come on, guys; let's try my house."

Billy's mother had communicated volumes. Her peace and quiet were more important to her than her son. She may not have meant to communicate that fact, but this is what Billy saw as he tried to hide his hurt. Her view of his relative importance was being communicated to him. In contrast Billy knew his mother would never communicate with her adult neighbors in that same tone of voice. Tragically, she had done more than rid herself of some rowdy boys; she had placed another minus in the mosaic of Billy's life.

Contrast this behavior with the example Jesus showed in Mark 10. The Saviour had just finished a lengthy discourse to the Pharisees and the disciples on God's views of divorce.

Sometime later they were interrupted by the presence of children. The disciples were irritated. Jesus expressed His displeasure to the disciples, reached down and drew the children to Him. You can imagine how those youngsters felt. They were important. From God's perspective, all people, young or old, are always of supreme importance.

To be like God is to love people. It has nothing to do with your personality. By temperament you may be a vivacious, people-centered person, or you may be a recluse. You may naturally gravitate toward the crowds or toward solitude. But if you want to be like God, you must be involved with people.

Place of the Home

It is interesting to note in Scripture the place of the home in ministering to people. Frequently, we find Jesus in people's homes. One day He was in the home of Zaccheus, another day He was with Simon the Pharisee. He frequented the home of His good friends Mary, Martha, and Lazarus. The roof of one home was even demolished as people clamored to get near Him.

Paul gives us an interesting glimpse into the lifestyle of Stephanas. His family was addicted to the ministry of people.

> I beseech you, brethren, (ye know the house of Stephanas, that it is the firstfruits of Achaia, and that they have addicted themselves to the ministry of the saints), (1 Cor. 16:15, KJV).

Here are some ideas on how you can use your home for the ministry:

1. Think of your church as a place to meet strangers whom you can entertain in your home. John and Elizabeth are perfect examples of this. I was a student in their small town and every restaurant was closed on Sundays. With no place to eat, I spent many Lord's Days fasting—not out of conviction but out of necessity. After church one Sunday, John and Elizabeth greeted me and asked if I had moved into their community.

Without hesitation they invited me home for dinner when they learned I was a student at the college nearby. When I arrived at their home, I noticed that the table was all ready; there was a place for me. Puzzled by this, I asked how they knew I was coming. Laughing, they said they didn't know. It was their habit to set an extra place every Sunday morning in anticipation of the stranger who would be joining them.

2. Volunteer to have missionaries who are on furlough into your home. Your pastor will be delighted to inform you about the schedules of your church's missionaries. This kind of exposure to your children will pay rich dividends. Your family will be exposed to godly, dedicated people of the faith, who will share some of the exciting things God is doing around the world.

A good friend of ours grew up in Chicago. His father taught at Moody Bible Institute and often invited God's people to share their home. This friend has commented on the strategic role that this has played in his life.

3. Make use of the holidays for serving others. You can make holidays people days. Invite them into your home to share with you the bounty of God's blessing. For example, try to include the widows, orphans, and others who experience a lack of family. They hold a special place in the heart of God. Over and over the Scriptures urge us to remember them.

Widows and widowers can be a double blessing to your family if the children's grandparents are not nearby. For them to see the mellowness and wisdom of age is an important ingredient in the discipling process of children. It teaches them respect and exposes them to a storehouse of experiences.

4. Make your home the neighborhood oasis. Encourage your children to bring their friends home. There are a lot of inexpensive games that can be kept handy and ready to use, and that will help make your home *the* place to come. Have a ready supply of freshly baked goodies. Your hospitality will make your children's friends more interested in the Gospel. Pray with your children for their friends; help them to see that the home is a good place for ministry.

Allow the neighborhood children to see incarnational Christianity. A friend of ours fixed up his basement and installed all kinds of games. This resulted in natural opportunities for leading some of the neighborhood children to Christ. Their family called it their "soul-trap." The home can serve a dual function as far as the ministry is concerned. It can be a tremendous vehicle in propagating the Gospel to the neighborhood, and it can serve as a schoolroom for your children as they learn from you what discipleship is all about.

Ideas for the Ministry

Ministering together as a family unit can be an exciting experience. It takes Christianity off the dusty shelves of academia and puts shoe leather on it. As you and your children minister together, they will be able to see that sharing the Gospel is more than handing out tracts—it is a lifestyle.

There are many creative things that you as a family can do together in proclaiming the Good News. The following are some that my wife and I have seen in action and commend to you:

Bridge building. Joe, Maggie, and their son thought up a neat idea on how to minister to their neighborhood. They borrowed a 16mm movie projector from their church and rented a Walt Disney movie. On the church mimeograph machine, they printed invitations inviting the neighborhood—young and old alike—to a party at their home. Their son was as excited about it as they were, as he roared all over the neighborhood and passed out the flyers. They rented an old-fashioned popcorn popper, and dozens of the neighbors came to sit on the back lawn, eat popcorn, and watch the movie.

They didn't try to evangelize that night. They wanted it to be a bridge-building time. Barriers were broken down, making it possible to have some of the neighbors over in a more intimate situation later on, when spiritual things could be discussed more naturally.

Evangelistic dinners formed the illustration used in the opening of this chapter. Let's go into more of the details. Art and Nancy DeMoss of Philadelphia first introduced us to this idea: Develop a list of prospective guests. It isn't necessary to know the people. Names can be obtained from neighborhood homeowner's association lists, newspapers, country clubs, etc. Invite an out-of-town speaker who is *not* a professional Christian worker but who would have public appeal. Print formal invitations inviting your guests to dinner and to hear the speaker. Mention something about Christianity on the invitations, either in the title of the speaker's talk or in the brief description of the speaker, so the guests will know that the evening will include something religious. About 25 percent of those invited will come. Every part of the preparation and presentation involves an opportunity for the children to be involved. As they pray and watch people respond, they have the opportunity to see God at work in the lives of people.

Something special. Invite another family to join you for a barbecue in the backyard or a picnic at some out-of-the-ordinary spot. You may want to do it on some special day such as the Fourth of July, Valentine's Day, Thanksgiving, or Easter. Another possibility is the birthday of one of your neighbors.

Don't feel you must preach the Gospel to them when you are together. Your objective is to create relationships with non-Christians. After your friendships are established, God will open doors of opportunity for you to share your faith.

Rest homes. Many elderly people in rest homes are forgotten. A visit from your family unit can be a breath of fresh air. You may want to form a small Gospel team. If you are musically inclined, you can present some musical numbers. Groups are encouraged to visit and minister on a regular basis in most nursing homes.

Most of the elderly people in situations like this rarely see children and would welcome the opportunity to interact with

98 / How to Disciple Your Children

them. You may find it helpful to prepare your children on how to respond to the elderly. There are some very sad scenes in store for them and they need to understand some of the problems of old age.

Often during these times, you are able to share your faith and leave some Christian literature. The children can join in sharing their faith through the use of hand puppets, singing, and even role playing of Bible characters. Plan together with them on how to make these times creative.

Friendship Evangelism

Jesus was the Friend of publicans and sinners. This was friendship evangelism. As relationships were established, people could see in the Saviour a quality of life that was attractive. This was the foundation upon which a commitment was built.

When we talk about ministering as a family, this is what we have in mind. Some call it *incarnational evangelism.* It involves leaving the cocoon of the Christian fellowship and building friendships with those still uncommitted to the Christian faith. Begin by asking yourselves as a family, "How many non-Christians consider us to be their good friends?" If the number is small, begin moving in the direction of establishing close friendships with non-Christians.

For many believers, friendship with publicans and unbelievers is not easy. There is a lack of commonality. They do not enjoy associating with people who dance, smoke, drink, and swear. Yet this is what the ministry is all about—following Jesus' example of becoming the Friend of publicans and sinners and introducing them to the Author of life.

11

Education in the Discipling Process

The word for *education* in the Old Testament means "to train." We see it in the familiar proverb of Solomon: "Train a child in the way he should go, and when he is old he will not turn from it" (Prov. 22:6).

Education in those ancient biblical days did not have as its objective merely teaching people how to make a living, but concerned itself further with character formation. Knowing could not be divorced from being and doing. The focal point was always a proper relationship with God.

In the early days of Israel's history, two things kept the home the center of learning. First was the fact that the Jews were an agrarian people. They did not live in cities, where the development of school systems would have been possible, but they lived on farms. Second, the writings of the first five books of the Old Testament—commonly known as the *Torah*—were painstakingly handprinted on large scrolls. Thus there were few copies available. Books of other types were even more scarce.

Instruction was done by word of mouth. Oral teaching illustrated by parental example was their method. The home was the only school and the parents the only teachers.

Moses understood the indispensable role of the family when he admonished Israel:

Only be careful, and watch yourselves closely so that you do not forget the things your eyes have seen or let them slip from your heart as long as you live. Teach them to your children and to their children after them (Deut. 4:9).

He felt the point to be sufficiently important to repeat it again and again in Deuteronomy:

These commandments that I give you today are to be upon your hearts. Impress them on your children. Talk about them when you sit at home and when you walk along the road, when you lie down and when you get up (Deut. 6:6-7).
Teach them to your children, talking about them when you sit at home and when you walk along the road, when you lie down and when you get up (Deut. 11:19).

First the tabernacle and later the temple was the center of worship for Israel. But its remoteness to the large majority of people made the home the location where training took place. Through the life-philosophy of the parents, God's teachings became imperishable. Through the purity and serenity of the Scriptures, fleshed out in the parents, God's teachings were made attractive. Because of the example of their parents' lives and the single-mindedness of their purpose, the children wanted to follow God.

When Israel went into Babylonian exile and their temple was destroyed, the synagogue evolved as the center of worship, education, and community government. There were many synagogues scattered throughout the Jewish communities. None of them had an altar or became a place of sacrifice. Neither did they replace the home as the chief institution for educating their children. The synagogue was merely viewed by the Israelites as an augmentation in the training process.

From a biblical perspective, the education of children, whether it be secular or spiritual, is the responsibility of parents. In modern times families have moved farther and farther away from this view. As parents surrender their responsibility in educating their children, the state moves in to fill the gap. Increasingly, "freedom of religion" is seen to mean "freedom from religion." The results have been devastating.

Time magazine, in a report on education in the United States, quoted one of education's leaders: "All of us children of the 20th century know or should know, that there are no absolutes in human affairs."

The media join our educators in declaring that the only absolute in life (if it can be called an absolute) is self-actualization. This philosophy can be summarized in the statement, "Get all you can, can all you get, and poison the rest." God is removed from any personal involvement with man and people seem to primarily want others to get out of their way. The result is a generation of youth who are addicted to doing their own thing.

From every quarter people are screaming for their rights, but no one is asking, "What is right?" Many of today's young people appear to be oblivious to any sense of moral absolutes. They communicate a lack of responsibility.

The blame may be placed at a number of doorsteps but ultimately it is the parents' fault, for they have delegated to others that which is their basic responsibility. If the situation is ever to be righted, the exposure of their children to this kind of hostile environment must be countered by aggressive action on the part of parents. This means spending sufficient time with the children to lay a proper foundation in the biblical absolutes.

Discipling our children in this hostile environment has not proven all that successful. Children converted to Christ out of non-Christian homes are often more zealous toward the things of God than children from Christian homes. In our endeavor to addict our children to the Gospel of Jesus Christ, we often inoculate them. As the Prophet Hosea said, "They become halfbaked." (See Hosea 7:8, LB.)

We cannot conclude from this, however, that it is better for children to be raised in a non-Christian environment. Such reasoning is both unbiblical and fallacious. Rather we must learn how to use Christian education to our advantage.

What You Should Expect from Your School System

Whether parents opt for a secular or a Christian school, certain basic ingredients must be present if parents are not going to abdicate their God-given responsibility.

The most obvious ingredient is that *the school must be the glove of the parents' hand.* Here in the United States our forefathers understood this principle when they established neighborhood schools. Parents in a small geographical locale elected a school board who in turn hired the school administration and oversaw the curriculum. All of this was monitored by the Parent-Teacher Association.

Concern for equal opportunity among minorities led to increased government intervention. Integration required children being bused from their neighborhood schools to other parts of the city. As a parent I am not concerned with the length of time my child must be on a bus, or whether she sits next to a child whose skin is a different color. My overriding concern is that the school system has ceased to be sensitive to how I feel about the education of my children.

The education of children is a parental responsibility. The parent is the primary teacher. The school can never become anything more than an extension of the parent. Whom do I want to be that extension? Whom do I want to represent my wife and me in the training of our children?

These are the generic questions!

If you live in a situation where it is impossible for you to get the attention of your children's teachers; if they do not represent to your children your philosophy of life; then you have no option but to change schools.

It is imperative that parents and teachers work closely together. This means frequent communication between the two parties. In many homes, it is not so much that the teacher represents a fundamentally different philosophy of life. Rather, through neglect, the parents have not maintained communication with the teachers.

Whether your children attend a Christian or public school, invite the teachers into your home. Get to know them. Share your expectations and commitment to Christ. Let them know how you feel about the education of your children and the role you expect them to play.

The Goals of Education

There are three goals my wife and I have for our children as they proceed with their formal education. They are:

1. A desire to learn. A child is born with an inquisitive mind. He is eager to learn. Asking questions, exploring the unknown—these are natural components of a normal child. Unfortunately, parents and teachers often team together in squelching this innate drive so that by the time the child is midway through his basic education, he hates school.

Education isn't simply the imparting of knowledge—if this were all there was to it, we would need only to give the student a map to the public library. Education must integrate knowledge into life so that there is proper understanding and application.

When this process is completed, learning takes place and the child's appetite is whetted. Education cannot be considered successful if it does not include this desire to learn.

2. A discerning mind. Ours is an age in which truth and error are constantly intermingled. It is important that youngsters be able to sift through the cacophony of voices that vies for their allegiance and be able to identify truth.

There is a difference between wisdom and intelligence. Not all smart people are wise; and not all wise people are smart. A person can have an IQ bordering on genius, and not be discerning.

Evangelical Christianity is guilty of some shoddy thinking: People believe the right things for the wrong reasons; others believe the wrong things for the right reasons. Our job is to teach our children to believe the right things for the right reasons!

3. *An understanding of where the student fits in the program of God.* Humanism, in seeking to exalt man, severs man's link with God. In so doing, man loses at least two things:

• *Man's uniqueness.* If he is not created in the image of God, he differs little from the animals. So why not practice abortion and euthanasia? It is done to horses and dogs. It is ironic that our legislators, in the same session of Congress, seek to enact laws controlling guns and allowing indiscriminate abortion.

• *Man's ability to understand God's world from God's point of view.* One of the tragedies of life is that people spend themselves on temporal values rather than on eternal values.

A proper value system, an appreciation of human worth, the realization that life is brief and that preparation must be made for eternity—these must be included in our goals of education.

Christian versus Non-Christian Schools

The secularization of our school system has resulted in a renewed interest in Christian schools. This in turn has generated a debate on the pros and cons of sending children to Christian schools.

There is no simple solution to this question. It is not so much the school but the environment that makes the difference. Often times Christian schools immunize our children. Filled with tremendous amounts of knowledge, they become desensitized to God's perspective on life. A while back, Youth for Christ did a study on children saturated in Christian education. These children lied, cheated, stole, and did all the other immoral things that non-churched children did—with the same degree of frequency. The churched kids had all the answers, but they weren't living them.

On the other hand, there are many fine Christian schools which blend academic excellence with an emphasis on applying the Scriptures.

Looking at secular schools, we see the same thing. Some have conditions that would make Sodom and Gomorrah blush. Others, although they have a bad environment, provide fine Christian support groups such as Youth for Christ, Young Life, and Campus Crusade.

Paul concludes his epistle to the Romans with these words: "I want you to be wise about what is good, and innocent about what is evil" (Rom. 16:19b). In our culture today, it is impossible to totally isolate our offspring from all evil, and it was the same in Paul's day. We can, however, augment our efforts in obeying this injunction by encouraging our children to identify with a good, positive Christian support group.

Need for Application of Christian Principles

The number one problem in evangelical Christianity today is application: there is much knowledge, but there are little life-changing results.

A pollster taking the spiritual temperature in America listed some impressive statistics on the number of people who attend church regularly, believe the Bible to be the Word of God, recognize the need for a conversion experience, etc. He concluded his report with words to this effect: "Never before in the history of the United States has the Gospel of Jesus Christ made such inroads while at the same time made so little difference on how people live." A more damning indictment could not be written on the church of Jesus Christ.

God is not pleased with a person in proportion to how holy he is. Rather He is pleased with a person in proportion to how holy he is as it relates to how much he knows. This is clearly seen when you contrast the harlot Rahab in the Old Testament with the scribes and Pharisees in the New Testament.

As you study Joshua 2, the Scriptures are very blunt in pointing out Rahab's moral imperfections. She was a harlot, a liar, a deceiver, and a traitor. She was willing to sell her own country into annihilation in order to save her own skin. Yet God exalted her as a woman of greatness.

In Matthew 1:5 she is included in the genealogy of our Lord and Saviour Jesus Christ. In Hebrews 11:31 we find her included in God's Hall of Fame. In James 2:25, when James wants an illustration of what proper works mingled with faith looks like, Rahab is his example.

Our moral sensibilities are offended and we reel back in astonishment. Why did God do this? Our answer is found in the narrative of Joshua 2. Years earlier (probably before Rahab's birth), word came to Jericho that the God of Israel had destroyed the mighty armies of Egypt.

Shortly afterward Israel dropped off the pages of history, spending 40 years wandering in the wilderness. All of a sudden, two of these Israelites appeared in Rahab's brothel. She was willing to risk everything she considered precious on the basis of a rumor over 40 years old. She was willing to act on the basis of very little information. When God saw this, He leaped over Rahab's moral flaws and exalted her.

Contrast her with the scribes and Pharisees in the day of the Lord Jesus. With no group was Jesus more harsh than these religious leaders. Their problem was the opposite of Rahab's. They had acquired great quantities of knowledge but made very little application. It is not how much you know that delights the heart of God. Rather it is what you do with what you know.

Holiness is absolute in that God is absolutely holy. His delight in His children, however, is not based on the degree to which they are absolutely holy, but on the degree to which they apply what they know. The Pharisees, relatively speaking, were more holy than Rahab. Their lifestyle was far more holy than hers, and yet Rahab was great in God's sight while the Pharisees were condemned. It is impossible to understand this without introducing the ingredient of application. The Pharisees were not nearly as holy as they ought to have been on the basis of what they knew. Rahab with all of her faults knew very little. But what she knew she applied.

The Challenge of Christian Education
God did not give His people the Word of God to make them smarter sinners. He gave it to them to make them holy saints. In

this regard Rahab is our heroine. God is looking for people like her who apply what they know.

It is precisely here that a parent faces his greatest challenge in discipling his children. Let me illustrate from personal experience. I became a Christian at 19 years of age, knowing next to nothing about the Bible. I had a great deal of experience and very little understanding. My challenge was to increase my knowledge.

My children, on the other hand, were born and are being raised in a Christian home. They attend a Christian school five days a week and church on Sunday. They have lots of knowledge and very little experience. Their challenge is to increase their experience.

My children and I both need application, but the need comes from different backgrounds. Because they know more than they have lived, application takes on an extra challenge. Not only must I help them experience what they know, I must also help them add the dimension of application.

Moses anticipated this need when he instructed Israel to relate the Word of God to the totality of their experience, namely, "Impress them [the commandments] on your children. Talk about them when you sit at home and when you walk along the road, when you lie down and when you get up" (Deut. 6:7).

The richest times spiritually that I have had with my children have centered around the application of Scriptures to the traumas of their lives. Adverse circumstances mar my children's happiness as people do not meet their expectations. My children know the Scriptures. What they need is guidance on how to apply the Scriptures to these experiences.

I remember well the day my son came home from school and announced that he not only did not like his new teacher, he was afraid of him. He pleaded to have his classes changed. After talking it over and discussing the details, my wife told him she would go to school and learn the teacher's point of view. But first, the two of them would thank the Lord for the situation and seek His wisdom. Our son replied, "How can I thank the Lord when I'm not thankful?" My wife suggested that maybe he could ask the Lord to make him *willing* to be thankful and so he began his prayer at that point.

The next day the teacher gave my wife his set of reasons why our son was placed in his class. They were valid, but the teacher was willing to change him to another class if she insisted. But my wife, not willing to make a decision until she was sure God was in it, went back to talk it over with our son.

His response was one of caution. He would wait a few days and pray about it. On the one hand he wanted to change classes; on the other hand he wanted to do what God wanted. He best expressed it when he said, "I want to do what the Lord wants, but I want His will to be what I want." I thought at the time, *this is where most Christians live.*

As time passed he was able to thank the Lord for his teacher and for being in that class. When the day arrived on which he had to make the final decision, he decided to stay where he had been placed. Long before the end of the school year, the teacher became his good friend. Even to the present he remembers that experience of wrestling through submission to the Lord's will and finding it good, acceptable, and perfect. The application of Scripture to daily experiences is the best education our children can find.

Our Primary Responsibility

In the maturation process, God brings into each individual's life a multiplicity of influences. One influence may be a godly grandmother who prays daily for him followed by contact with Child Evangelism or some camping program. The Sunday School teacher may have a part as well as the youth pastor. A Christian teacher in the school system or a Young Life leader may contribute. It is a matrix of ministries that God brings into each person's life to help him toward spiritual maturity.

There are so few people who are willing to invest in the lives of others that when the Lord brings such a person into the life of one of our children, cherish that person as a co-laborer in the

Lord. There are so many influences in a secular society that seek to proselytize our children, it is imperative that as parents we assume the primary responsibility to educate our children. We may delegate certain aspects of it to others, but we dare not surrender this God-given task as primarily ours.

12
Setting Family Goals

A goal is something you want to accomplish stated in measurable terms. The Christian's goals are an expression of what he understands to be the will of God.

Dr. Luke records the conversion of Saul the Pharisee in Acts 9. In his encounter with the Lord, Saul asked these questions: "Who art Thou, Lord?" (v. 5) and "Lord, what wilt Thou have me to do?" (v. 6, KJV) These are the two foundational questions for every conscientious believer.

A person clearly defining his goals should ask three questions:

- Where am I going?
- How am I going to get there?
- How will I know when I have arrived?

These three questions may be asked in a variety of ways, but the intent is always the same. For example, say you want to set some goals on the basis of Saul's second question in Acts 9:6, KJV: "What wilt Thou have me to do?" Stated in terms of a goal the three questions are:

- What does the Lord want me to do?
- How does the Lord want me to do it?
- How will I know when it is done?

Let us use another example: you and your spouse are praying about how your daughter should spend her summer. The writer of an ancient proverb says, "He who aims at nothing hits it." You as parents are concerned, but the more ill-defined your goal for your daughter, the less chance you have of her reaching it. So together you ask these three questions:

- What does she need?
- How can she get it?
- How will we know when she has it?

Let us analyze these three questions one more time to see what we have:

What does she need? This brings focus to the desired result or the goal itself.

How can she get it? This outlines the activities in which she will engage as she moves toward the goal.

How will we know when she has it? This calls attention to the evaluation process as we look back to see if the goal was accomplished.

Knowing the Will of God

Goal-setting is simply verbalizing what you believe to be God's will for your life. When you say, "The will of God is for me to move to another city," that becomes your goal. But how do you know it is the will of God for you to do something? How do you know that your goals are not the product of your own desires?

Let us begin by noting that there are two categories of things we call the will of God:

1. Those things He has stated in the Bible. We will call these the *objective* indicators of God's will. For example, the Apostle Paul says, "It is God's will that you should be holy" (1 Thes.

4:3). All the commands in Scripture express God's will for our lives—things like prayer, letting the Word of God richly dwell in us, sexual purity, and loving our neighbors.

2. *Those things not specifically stated in the Bible, but which we feel prompted by the Holy Spirit to do.* We will call these the *subjective* indicators of God's will. Take for example your initial decision to marry your beloved. How did you know it was God's will? It was a subjective decision based on how you felt God was leading. Most of the decisions we make in life fit under this second category. Remember, the Holy Spirit never subjectively leads a person to do what the Scriptures objectively prohibit.

Let us further note that we use the word *know* in more than one way. Scientifically, it is used to denote those things that we observe *after the fact*. Take a hypothetical interview with Wernher Von Braun, the rocket expert, as an example. If you asked him, in an interview prior to the first manned space flight to the moon, "Dr. Von Braun, do you *know* that the astronauts will safely land on the moon and then safely return?" He would quickly answer that he did not *know* for sure. Elaborate tests had been run. To the best of their ability, they had minimized the risks. But no, they would not *know* that the astronauts would return safely until *after* they returned.

The other way we use *know* is to communicate things seen through the eyes of faith. They may be in the future, but God promises them in the Scriptures. As Christians we say that we *know* we will go to heaven when we die. We do not *know* it in the scientific sense of the word, since it is yet to happen, but we do *know* it from the perspective of faith. The Apostle Paul writes: "And we know that in all things God works for the good of those who love Him, who have been called according to His purpose" (Rom. 8:28). He uses *know* in the sense of what faith tells him. He trusts the character of God, and on the basis of that says he *knows* all things work together for good.

When we say, "I know that the will of God is . . ." what do we mean? If we are talking about what God has *objectively* said in His Word, then we mean that we *know* it through the eyes of faith, but it is faith placed in an objective standard that has stood the test of the centuries.

If, however, we are talking about what God has *subjectively* revealed to us through His Spirit, then we mean that we don't really *know* it any more than Von Braun *knows* that the astronauts will return safely before it happens. For both of us it is risk-taking pure and simple.

Many Christians become confused on this issue. They walk around in a fog asking, "How can we know the will of God?" Because they use the word *know* most of the time in the objective sense of the term, it never occurs to them that they cannot use it in the same way when referring to being led by the Holy Spirit. There is no way they can eliminate the element of risk.

Taking risks is another way of saying, "walking by faith." Faith can be defined as *commitment before knowledge.* On Mt. Carmel, Elijah took his sacrifice and drenched it with water before asking God to set it ablaze with a fire from heaven. Elijah did not *know* God would do it until he saw the altar consumed. He believed God would do it and took the appropriate risk. That is a biblical illustration of *faith.*

As you read through Hebrews 11, you will note that faith is always referred to in dimensions of the *future* and the *invisible* (Heb. 11:1). These heroes of the faith committed themselves before they knew all the facts. This is risk-taking. This is faith!

If it is true then, that you cannot *know* the will of God in the *subjective* sense of being led by the Holy Spirit—if you must walk by faith—is there some way that you can minimize the risk? Von Braun could not eliminate the risk, but he did everything in his power to minimize it through an elaborate system of tests and checks.

Is there any way that you as a Christian can minimize the risk factor as you step out to do what you believe to be the will of God? Yes, there is a system of tests and checks that can help in determining the will of God. They are not foolproof. You still must walk by faith. But they are biblical guides to help you.

1. Submission. You begin with an attitude of neutrality. Whatever the desire, lay it before the Lord and surrender to His perfect will. Until you unwrap your fingers from around the desire and give it to God—until you can say, "Your will, not my will be done"—you aren't ready to know the will of God.

2. Word of God. How do the Scriptures enlighten you on the subject? Begin by checking in the Word of God to see if the issue is referred to. God has given you His Word to help you know His will. The psalmist says, "Your Word is a lamp to my feet and a light for my path" (Ps. 119:105).

3. Counsel. Solomon says, "In the multitude of counselors there is safety" (Prov. 11:14, KJV). A wise Christian will follow the counsel of proven men. Be careful that you don't pick counselors that you know will confirm you in your prejudices.

4. Peace. One of the indicators of the Holy Spirit's leading is peace. His will is accompanied by an inner quietness and assurance. Isaiah says, "And the work of righteousness shall be peace; and the effect of righteousness, quietness, and assurance forever" (32:17, KJV).

5. Circumstances. This is one of the most objective ways God uses in leading His children. You pray about whether to buy a particular house or not, and as you pray someone else buys it. The will of God has been revealed (Rom. 8:28).

All five of these guides are gracious ways God uses to assist His children in knowing His will—without negating the need to walk by faith. All five, of course, presuppose an attitude of prayer. As you pray the Holy Spirit leads.

Evaluating Your Goals

We stated earlier that goal-setting is another way of stating what we believe to be the will of God. There are, however, different kinds of goals and these must be clearly distinguished and understood when evaluating progress.

1. Controllable versus uncontrollable. It is possible to control the results of some goals and impossible to control the results of others. For the sake of illustration, let us say you feel it is the will of God in the course of the next 12 months to: (1) memorize the Book of Philippians and (2) talk with every neighbor on the block. These two goals are well within your control. Barring a catastrophe, you decide the degree to which they are to be met.

Now let us imply you have two other goals. They are: (1) 16 people will come to Christ through your ministry in the next 12 months, and (2) your Sunday School class will increase in number by 50 percent. These may be legitimate goals but they are beyond your control. For example, you don't convert people. And for your Sunday School class to grow would involve the cooperation of the entire class.

2. Quality versus quantity. Some goals are qualitative in nature and others are quantitative. An illustration of a *qualitative* goal might be that in the next year you are going to work on controlling your temper. The Holy Spirit has convicted you in this area and you vow to make improvement.

If you travel a great deal, you may sense the need to spend more time with your son. So you set as a *quantitative* goal that you will take your son with you on three of your trips over the next 12 months.

Evaluating qualitative goals is far more difficult than evaluating quantitative goals. This is especially true when it comes to the character of a person. A man may be able to evaluate the quality of an automobile as it comes off the assembly line. To evaluate the quality of his child's commitment to Christ, however, is an elusive if not impossible task.

3. Goals for yourself versus goals for others. Some of your goals are directed at your own performance and some are directed at the performance of others. As you seek to bring your life into conformity with Christ, you ask the Holy Spirit to reveal areas in which He would have you major. Such goals may have to do with your prayer life, how you relate to your family, your time spent in the study of the Scriptures, and so on. These are all goals you set for yourself as you respond to the leadership of the Holy Spirit.

Then there are goals that you establish for others. You may, for example, have a goal for your secretary. Or you and your spouse may set some goals for your children. Examples of goals you might set for your children would be to have a quiet time every day, to read C.S. Lewis' *Chronicles of Narnia* (Macmillan), or to have your children do something as mundane as straightening their room every morning before school.

Up to this point it has been fairly easy to distinguish the various kinds of goals. What is not so easy is how to evaluate them as they are incorporated into our lives. For the sake of illustration, let us talk about what we believe to be the will of God for our children.

If we are not going to frustrate both ourselves and our children, we will have to carefully think through the kinds of goals we will set for them. In an earlier chapter, we talked about expectations and disappointments. Our expectations and disappointments are nowhere more glaringly revealed than in how we handle what we feel is God's will for our children's lives. As we set goals for our children, we need to ask ourselves these questions:

- Are the goals controllable or uncontrollable?
- Are they qualitative or quantitative in nature?
- Do we have our children's agreement that these goals are something they should work on or are these goals solely our ideas?

In an earlier chapter, positive and negative commandments were discussed. Positive commandments are qualitative in nature and impossible to measure. This chapter opened by defining a goal as "something you want to accomplish stated in measurable terms." In your own life you may choose as a goal one of the positive commandments—such an example would be to love your wife. Because you cannot measure this goal, you may elect to apply it in more specific terms. For example:

- I will plan a date with my wife at least once a week.
- I will remember special occasions with a card.
- I will tell her at least once a day that I love her.
- I will help her with the dishes three nights a week.

You may conclude that the Lord would have you do these four things as a visible expression of your love for your wife.

Evaluating qualitative goals that you have made for yourself is both difficult and subjective. Evaluating such goals in the lives of your children is impossible. Efforts to do so will disrupt the family unit. The following reference illustrates this: Jesus said, "If you continue in My word, then are you My disciples indeed" (John 8:31, KJV). As you disciple your children, it is imperative that they learn and obey the Word. You lead the way in making it one of their goals. It is a positive commandment. So you decide to make the goal specific and outline a plan for your child. For instance:

- Memorize three verses per week.
- Read through the Bible once a year.
- Spend three hours per week in Bible study.

Now let us observe what can happen.

1. Because my child has done these things, it does not necessarily follow that he is continuing in the Word. He may be like the Pharisees and refuse to apply what he knows.

2. Nowhere in the Bible does it say that my child has to do the above three things in order to continue in the Word. These are my standards, not the Bible's.

3. These goals are mine, not my child's. They result in my developing expectations of him that are unrealistic.

All of this means that you must be very careful when setting goals for your children. They can so easily produce the opposite results of what you had in mind for them.

Particularly as they get older, allow your children to set their own goals. Remember, faith is risk-taking and risk-taking is impossible to avoid in doing the will of God. Risk-taking implies the possibility of failure. One of the greatest heritages you can give your children is to create an environment in which they are free to fail.

We're not talking about the kind of failure that a person

experiences when he willfully transgresses the commandments of God. Rather it is the failure that comes from launching out into the unknown. Allow your young disciple to take risks with God. Let him agonize through the process of determining God's will and setting appropriate goals for himself.

Here's a theoretical situation: your teenage daughter has an opportunity to spend her summer in a church mission program. If she accepts, it means she cannot earn money for her college education. Next year is her senior year in high school and there are many things she is going to want to do that cost money. Should she go with the church group and trust God for her finances or should she go to work?

She comes to you with her options. Instead of telling her what to do, you review with her the five guidelines in determining God's will—submission, the Word, counsel, peace, and circumstances. Then the decision is hers. She agonizes over it. Only as she looks in retrospect will she know if her expectations were met. This is involved in the process of making disciples.

Conclusion

For the Christian, risk-taking is done against the backdrop of God's grace. God's commitment to His own is unconditional. It is not based on performance or reciprocity. We are willing to take those risks that are intrinsic to faith because we know He is committed to us and has our best interests in His plan: "If God is for us, who can be against us?" (Rom. 8:31)

One of the marks of a person who understands the grace of God is his sense of dependence upon God. Not only does his spiritual bankruptcy drive him to the Cross, he recognizes that self-effort is not sufficient in the Christian life. This desperate dependence upon God's grace is nowhere more keenly needed than in the discipling of his children. The more he gets involved in the task, the more dependent he feels.

They are our children but they are God's disciples. As parents we are willing to hold them with an open hand and take risks with them because of this fact.

Paul, in evaluating a challenging situation, cried out, "And who is equal to such a task?" (2 Cor. 2:16)

Crisp and clear is God's answer: "My grace is sufficient for you, for My power is made perfect in weakness" (2 Cor. 12:9). What more could we ask for as we face our most important job with joy?